When I picked the book up, I though
the parts about the magical 2007 s
Kramer at Fairless. Three hours later I was still reading, and I realized
that every parent should read this book to gain an appreciation for the
things a coach does to provide a quality program for their sons and
daughters.

-Jim Jennings
Father of Former Fairless player Jordan Jennings

The recently published book, *The Best-Laid Plans of a High School
Basketball CEO*, was co-authored by two Ohio high school basketball
coaches. One of the authors, Randy Montgomery (North Canton
Hoover), is arguably among the best high school coaches in the state.
The other coach, Matt Kramer (Fairless and Canton South), was
extremely successful at Navarre Fairless and then moved to Canton
South, where he had to face many issues the average high school coach
must deal with on a regular basis. The book presents a very good
overview of how to decide what job is a "good" one or a good match for
the coach, picking a staff, promoting your program, off-season programs, team discipline, etc. There are many good ideas in this book,
which is a great blueprint for success, but the part I found most interesting, and potentially most helpful, were the sections about dealing
with adversity, lack of administrative support and, eventually, being
non-renewed or fired from a coaching position. The foreword for the
book was written by West Virginia University coach, Bob Huggins, and
there are testimonials from Dean Chance (1964 Cy Young Award MLB
Pitcher and an All-Ohio basketball player who led his high school team,
West Salem Northwestern, to a state championship), and Brad
Brownell, the current head coach at Clemson University. I would
highly recommend this book.

-Frank Jessie
Former Assistant Coach
University of Cincinnati

The Best-Laid Plans
of a High School Basketball CEO:

A Coach's Guide to Seeking & Securing,
Building & Maintaining a Successful Program

Matt Kramer & Randy Montgomery

First published by Dog Ear Publishing
4010 W. 86th Street, Ste H
Indianapolis, IN 46268
www.dogearpublishing.net

ISBN: 978-1-4575-0808-0

This book is printed on acid-free paper.

Printed in the United States of America

Table of Contents

Foreword by Bob Huggins

Foreword

RANDY AND MATT have put together a great book for building a public high school basketball program. Randy was on my original staff at Walsh College (now Walsh University) back in the early 1980's, so I have known him for over thirty years in coaching and as a friend.

At Walsh, Randy worked closely with me to build that program into an NAIA power before he moved on to build two great high school programs of his own at Wooster Triway and North Canton Hoover. The ideas he shares in these pages—the ones he used to reach two Final Fours—are perhaps the best plans for running a successful high school basketball program at a public school anywhere in print.

Matt adds the unique perspective of a younger head coach who has worked to rebuild two high school programs: Navarre Fairless and Canton South. Although his situations have presented different challenges, his ideas—specifically the ones he used to lead Fairless to a "Sweet-16"—team closely with Randy's on leading a basketball program.

The Best-Laid Plans of a High School Basketball CEO offers many great coaching and leadership ideas that have been tested over the years by two successful high school coaches. I highly recommend it not only for all basketball coaches working in programs across the country, but also for coaches in all sports and leaders of young people.

-Bob Huggins
Head Men's Basketball Coach
West Virginia University

1
Evolution of the Premise

As the last of my players trudged out of the locker room, two dusky rays from high in the Canton Memorial Field House rafters cut through the silent darkness, casting a surreal spotlight at the center of the court where ninety minutes earlier there had been pandemonium—an unbridled celebration three years in the making. Some of the silence from my usually lively group was indicative of exhaustion—physical and emotional. But it was also a product of the fact that all of us were still trying to comprehend the fact that we had been a part of perhaps *the* most dramatic ending in the history of *any* high school basketball championship game this side of *Hoosiers*.

I know that sounds like hyperbole, but I have spoken to hundreds of people who witnessed that game on March 10, 2007—some I know very well and some complete strangers—and a majority say it was the most extraordinary ending to any game they have ever seen. Of course the readers can ultimately decide the game's place in the annals of dramatic endings when they read the specifics later in the book—or they can go to *You Tube* and watch the last 30 seconds of overtime and decide now. Either way, that's not really the point to sharing the story. In retrospect, the trip we earned on that night to Ohio's Division-II "Sweet 16" was actually secondary to what came next.

Dragging our feet across the court toward the exit that led to our team bus, the entire group—players and coaches—stopped in unison at center court as if some unseen force within the dim rays of light were holding us there. At first everyone seemed to simply be taking one final look around the arena we had just conquered; then, the moment turned into one of the most special I have ever spent as the *leader* of a program.

As the rest of us huddled, bent down on one knee, held hands, and bowed our heads, Mike Husted—my assistant in charge of our post players, one of my best friends in the world and a minister by trade—offered an impromptu offering of thanks. The half-court prayer was not witnessed by anyone outside of our basketball family—with the possible exception of a custodian working in the recesses of the upper deck of the two-tiered venerable Field House—but it was one of the most authentically spiritual experiences of my life. Here was a group of 'average kids' who had fought through a rebuilding project—one that included two seasons of struggling that would have caused many high school athletes to find a new hobby—and stuck together to realize a great vision. The moment was anything *but* average.

Yes, the winning *was* intoxicating, but I knew something much stronger than winning had brought us to that moment. It was the relationships we had built and the growth of the players into young men during the journey that turned the night into a script straight from heaven. For the first time in my career, I fully realized the gravity of my responsibility as the leader of a public high school basketball program.

As we broke our 'family' huddle and continued to the exit, my top assistant—and one of my best friends in the world—Tim Vick said, "Matt, you blew it. You should have written a book about how you rebuilt this program, because tonight would have been the perfect ending."

Little did Tim know it then, but his comment was the perfect push at the perfect time. It was a real-life rags-to-riches story—complete with the made-for-television ending—leading to an era of success born out of the hard work and perseverance of *hometown* kids that truly lifted an entire community. With that little push from Tim Vick, I decided to go to work in the spring of 2007 organizing years of self-reflective writing with the idea that I would, perhaps, write a book.

Early in the process, I realized there wouldn't be much of an audience *outside* the Fairless community for a book solely about my 2007 team's '*Rockyesque*' rise to a "Sweet-16". Likewise, I knew I didn't have a surefire formula for rebuilding *every* public high school basketball program. Regardless, I held firmly to the idea there *was* a book idea somewhere in the experience that would be compelling to other leaders, so I pressed on and sought to find it.

As I continued my work, I had many people ask me—including friends and family—what made me think my book could be successful. Since I had never written to please anyone but myself, I didn't initially have an answer to that question; upon thinking it through, here's what I came up with:

During my career I have read every book that was written by the legendary John Wooden. I have studied and digested the words in books written by my favorite coach—former Chicago Bulls and Los Angeles Lakers coach Phil Jackson. I have read Dean Smith's words,

Mike Krzyzewski's words, and the words of countless other *world-famous* coaches from a variety of sports—all of whom coached, or are now coaching, on a much grander stage than one upon which I am *ever* likely to coach.

Every one of the coaches I have read is amazing in his accomplishments and contributions to his respective professional or collegiate sports, and I have gained many insights from the words they put in print. But they are also coaching in a *far* different environment under a *completely* different set of dynamics than the ones under which I operate as a *public* high school head basketball coach.

So here's the question: Where is the book written by a public high school head basketball coach that is geared for someone like me—a book that gives advice and offers stories of experiences similar to mine for me to learn from—written by someone who is dealing with essentially the same rules and circumstances with which I deal? The answer to that question was simple: There really is no such book.

So I set out to write a book that would be *useful* for coaches working in *public school programs* all over the country—from head high school coach on down to those important people who coach in youth programs. My initial vision had me *pushing* the text toward a how-to manual, and I felt like my eight years as a head coach—at the time I started this project— and my ten years as an assistant had lent me plenty of relevant experiences to share. But I also knew that I didn't have *all* the answers. Undeterred, I continued to work on the framework of the book while I sought a way to make it a coaching and leadership read that would reach the masses. All along, the answer was right in front of me.

Enter Randy Montgomery, *legendary* Ohio high school boys' basketball coach. Randy is a man who elevated two dormant programs— Wooster Triway and North Canton Hoover—to *elite* status over a thirty-year coaching career that saw him eclipse the 500-win plateau in 2011. A highly accomplished coach who enjoys contributing to the game of basketball *beyond* the stellar work he has done with his own programs, Randy Montgomery was a professional role model I had always admired and tried to emulate from a distance as a young assistant coach.

In early January of 2001—my first season as a head coach—I got the chance to meet Randy when he brought his top-ranked and undefeated Triway team into the Fairless gym for a mid-season, non-conference game. My Fairless team had gotten off to a slow start, but we were improving and coming off of a last-second victory over our back-yard rival, Tuslaw. I felt the State of Ohio's top Division-II team would be a good gauge to see how far *we* had to go to become an elite program.

The answer I received that January night was as bitter as Ohio's winter weather—Triway beat us by thirty-five points, and it *felt* like it had been sixty.

After I addressed my players following that dose of reality and explained to them that we had just been beaten by a team that was likely to end the year ranked number one in the state—Triway did win the 2001 AP Division-II State Poll Championship by going 20-0—I walked through the coach's office that adjoined the visiting locker room to ours, and I caught Coach Montgomery as he was picking up his things to leave. I told him that night that I felt his program was *the* model program in the state and that I hoped to imitate much of what he was doing as I built *my* program at Fairless. I also thanked him for not hanging a fifty-point loss on us, because I felt he had been kind in keeping the margin at thirty-five.

That night, Randy told me he had scouted us enough to see that I was doing a good job of getting things started at Fairless. He told me that if *I* believed I was doing things the right way, the Fairless program would eventually do great things under my leadership—if I was willing to stick to my plan.

I appreciated the kind words from Randy but, because I didn't know him all that well, I didn't know how sincere he was. As that year wore on, Randy and I began to correspond via email to talk about common opponents, scouting reports, and all things related to running a basketball program. At first, we were simply colleagues talking basketball. But as time wore on, Randy became a mentor to me without even knowing he was mentoring me—and I realized his kind words the night our teams met had been as sincere as any I had ever heard from another coach.

Today he is a great friend who continues to be a fountain of coaching knowledge that I tap into on a regular basis. Years after the night I first met Randy Montgomery, the answer to fortifying this book with exactly what it needed to become a great read for all public school coaches was right at my fingertips, and I still didn't see it until it jumped off the computer screen and smacked me in the face.

In one of our email conversations toward the end of the 2009 season, Randy mentioned that he'd like to attempt to make a coaching video to share some of his experiences and ideas on how to run a program with other coaches because—in his words—*"I think I might have some good things to offer."*

You *think?* To me, Randy Montgomery is the top public school head basketball coach in the State of Ohio, and I believed that *long* before we became close friends. I *know* he has things to offer that would help *every* coach. When Randy told me that he wanted to try doing a video, I told him I was in the beginning stages of working on a book idea that might make a contribution to the coaching profession. Randy responded by telling me that he'd love to do something like write a book.

With a half-joking tone that was intended to read his feelings on the idea, I told him that he should co-author with me on *my* book idea. His response was typically humble Randy Montgomery: "I love the idea, but who in the world cares enough about *Randy Montgomery* or *Matt Kramer* to buy a book that we wrote?"

My response was exactly as follows: "Randy, I don't think anyone cares enough *specifically* about *Matt Kramer* to read a book just because *I* wrote it, but I do think my experience with successfully rebuilding a downtrodden program has merit, and I also believe that more people in the State of Ohio than you ever imagined would want to read the things *Randy Montgomery* has to say about running a basketball program— because everything you have touched in coaching has turned to gold."

I then stressed to him how helpful the things he had shared with me over the years had been to *my* career. I told him that if the things he had to offer were greatly beneficial to me, then they would also be help-ful to other coaches around the state, and even the country.

When we were done emailing that day—even though I could tell he wasn't sold on the idea—I could not let go of trying to find a way to get Randy involved. I whole-heartedly believed that putting Randy's time-tested expertise *with* my experiences was the key to bringing it all together.

After giving it some thought, I remembered a book I had read by Phil Jackson and Charlie Rosen called *More Than a Game*, a two-voice book that had offered me a great basketball *and* leadership reading experience. In *More Than a Game*, Mr. Rosen and Coach Jackson went back and forth from chapter to chapter sharing their basketball and career journeys in their writing. I thought that a similar back and forth between Randy Montgomery and me was the way to provide a rewarding reading experi-ence for a wide coaching and leadership audience. I felt I had found my premise, and I immediately pitched it to Coach Montgomery.

I told Randy that we would write the book together, sharing ideas and stories about topics related to leading a program—and leading young people. I told him his would be the '*Phil Jackson*' voice—the guy who had made two stops and been ultra-successful at both, piling up championships and wins, and doing it in his very own first-class, innovative manner; his **500-sections** would be centered on the ideas that led his programs to over *500* career victories, *seven* career "*Sweet-16*" appearances, two trips to the State of Ohio's *Final Four*, and *countless* league championships; his *part* would be to supply the voice of a leader who has mastered a profession that very few master—a coach with *Hall-of-Fame* credentials.

I told him mine would be the voice of a coach who has used many of the ideas in this book to eclipse 100 victories while rebuilding two struggling programs—a coach who has fought his way off of one 'hot seat' and one who was burned sitting on another. Therefore, I would *proudly* center my **100-sections** on the stories and process of leading my first program from the depths of losing to the magical memories on that March night in 2007 I have already begun to describe. But, it would also *candidly* focus on the experiences and circumstances that led to being cut short while attempting to do the same in my second head-coaching job—emphasizing that both results were wrought from hard work and *the best-laid plans.*

I told Randy that we would do what we always have done—talk basketball *and* leadership. But this time we would put the conversations into print with the idea that our stories and ideas could be helpful to other coaches and leaders.

When I explained this premise to Randy Montgomery the way I just explained it here, he was fully on board and the idea for a book was born. A little less than three years after I first started the project—in the fall of 2010—the first edition was put into print and titled *CEO: Coach, Educator, Organizer.*

We both *liked* it and felt like it could be a helpful read for coaches and leaders of young people. So we started small by putting a couple hundred copies into print in time for me to promote the original book at Coach Bob Huggins' coaching clinic at *West Virginia University* in October of 2010. Whereas the original copies *did* circulate pretty well, especially in the Canton area, I didn't want to just *like* it—I wanted to *love* it.

Therefore, I went back to work by listening to the feedback I was getting from coaches, players, fans and parents—and by reading the initial version. As I read, instead of trying to *push* the text into becoming a 'how-to' manual that had a magical message that would *sell* to the masses and teach every coach to win 500 games, I *listened* to the words and let them *lead* me where *they* were trying to go so *they* could *speak* to the masses.

In the end, the words clearly reminded me that every public school district presents different variables and challenges, leaving a leader only one thing he or she can be certain to control: a whole-hearted attempt at constructing *the best-laid plans*—which also led to the new title.

The Best-laid Plans of a High School Basketball CEO is a book that offers just what the title suggests—some of the ideas that a 500-win coach and a 100-win coach have used to lead public high school programs. But it also offers stories that show how those *best-laid plans* unfold—at times leading to sell-out crowds, championships and the coach receiving the key to the city; and other times how those same plans end in empty bleachers, sleepless nights and the athletic director collecting the coach's key to the gym. In both cases—and all those in between—our hope is that *The Best-laid Plans of a High School Basketball CEO* offers something useful for every leader who reads it...

Randy and I would like a young aspiring head coach who just graduated from college in Georgia to read this book and find ideas in it that help him or her begin shaping a coaching philosophy.

We would like a junior varsity coach in Kentucky to read it and realize how important his loyalty and work ethic are to the head coach for whom he works.

We would like a first-year head coach in Missouri to read our book and find something he never considered that he immediately uses to get his program rolling in the right direction.

We would like a veteran coach in Tennessee to take something from this book and use her own innovativeness to adapt it and make it a better fit for her program.

We'd like a coach in Delaware to learn something from one of the stories in this book that helps him sidestep a career land mine.

We would like a fourth-year head coach in Indiana who is sitting on a *'hot seat'*—feeling like he is coaching for his life—to read this book and find that someone else out there has gone through the difficulties he is experiencing, then realize he will come out of it a better coach—and a better person.

And *I* would like coaches everywhere who have been non-renewed—a euphemism for being fired—to find strength in the story I share about my experience with *non-renewal* so they may find the path to their bounce-back jobs.

Finally, after getting feedback from some of the parents of our athletes who read the first version, we stumbled across the idea that we would also like moms and dads all over the country to read our book and gain better insight into what the coaches in their school districts are doing to try and create the best in everything a program can offer their sons or daughters.

But mostly we want *all* coaches—male or female, no matter what level or what part of the country—to be able to put this book down after enjoying its ideas and stories, and feel like it makes them a part of the fraternity of coaches that uses *The Best-Laid Plans* to *lead* young people.

2

Beginnings in the Coaching Game:
No two paths are the same...

---

500 (Montgomery)

MANY OF THE ideas I share in this book, the ones I have implemented in my programs at Wooster Triway and North Canton Hoover, came from Salem and its legendary coach John Cabas. Salem was first-class high school basketball back in the 1960's and 1970's. It was typical small-town America—a tight-knit community that was far enough away from any major city that the high school sports teams were what shaped the community's identity. And in Salem, the main sport was basketball.

The population of the town was only 16,000, and the high school gym—sold out for every home game—held 4,000 people. So, literally, one-fourth of the town was in attendance on game nights. It was a tremendous high school basketball environment that captured my attention at a very young age.

Program promotion was unbelievable at Salem. When people went in the newspaper shop that sold our team's *Chuck Taylor Converse* shoes, they were really walking into a *Salem Quaker* team shop. There were schedule cards, bumper stickers, programs, and, most importantly, that shop was also a place where the community members could purchase their season tickets for *Quaker* home basketball games. For a young boy growing up in Salem, it was impossible to avoid wanting to be a *Salem Quaker* basketball player. That always stuck with me, and I have tried to create similar environments at Triway and Hoover in my coaching career.

When my brother—six years older than I—started to play for Salem, our family traveled everywhere he played, so I caught the 'basketball bug' at an early age. The packed houses at home games, the buzz about the team in the community, my brother starring for the team—everything I saw made me want to play basketball at Salem.

Once I was old enough to make the team, I found out every Salem player was treated in a first-class manner. During my high school career we ate steak dinners after *every* away game at Timberlane's, a fine food restaurant. We traveled by charter buses to road games when the trip was of significant length. We were given black blazers with a team emblem on them to wear to games and in school. The booster club fed us after home scrimmages, and we stayed in the best hotels when we would travel for preseason away scrimmages.

On the court, we played the best teams we could find. Our season ticket base was over 2,000; our pep band and cheerleaders were as good as it gets; and John Cabas could flat out coach and promote. We were the best show in town, and the community couldn't get enough *Quaker* basketball.

The experiences I had with basketball in Salem made me think that *every* high school basketball program did the things we did—I really did. But in talking to my teammates while playing at Youngstown State, I found out that *no* other schools did the things we did at Salem, and that really began to make me believe I could do great things in coaching.

After college I went to work at many summer basketball camps around the country to learn as much as I could—from as many successful coaches as I possibly could meet. I worked at the *Pocono Invitational Camp* in the Pocono Mountains, *Five-Star Basketball Camp*—which was *the* elite summer basketball camp back in the 70's. I also worked the *Bob Knight Basketball School* at *Indiana University* several times.

Coach Knight ran an incredible camp with stations *twice* a day to emphasize fundamental skill work, an emphasis that made a lasting impression on me before I ever coached a game. A coach worked his tail off at Coach Knight's camp, but it was also the highest *paying* camp I ever worked, and the chance to learn from a coach of Bobby Knight's caliber far surpassed any amount of summer money I might have been able to make.

Besides the camps I already mentioned, I worked a number of other camps over the years, including *Eastern Ohio Basketball Camp* under the direction of *Charlie Huggins*. Charlie was a legendary high school basketball coach in Ohio, winning three state titles. I felt working with the best coaches would be a prime way for me to learn how to coach basketball, and there was none better than Charlie Huggins.

Of course, Charlie is also the father of three very good former collegiate players: *Bob Huggins* played at West Virginia and has gone on to a legendary college coaching career at Cincinnati, briefly at Kansas State, and now back at his alma mater; Harry played Division-I ball for a period at Texas Christian University; and Larry Huggins starred at Ohio State in the 1980's with Clark Kellogg. And at the head of the family, Charlie Huggins was perhaps *the* greatest high school basketball coach in Ohio history. Larry, Harry, and Bob all played for their father, and all three won state titles under his direction. As a young coach, I wanted to hear all about those experiences, so I spent a significant amount of time with the Huggins family at their little 'basketball village' in Sherrodsville, Ohio.

The Eastern Ohio Basketball Camp is out in the middle of nowhere but, at *Eastern*, basketball has always been taught at the highest level. So many stories came out of that camp that it could make a great book in itself, but I will share just one to give an idea of the no-nonsense approach that was taken there.

One night at 10:02 p.m.—or two minutes after lights-out time— Larry, Harry, Bob and I were with some other coaches in the cafeteria talking hoops and eating ice cream. Some laughter and noise was coming from a *dorm*, which, back then, was really more of a barracks. Since we were in charge of the dorms after lights out, Bob, Larry, Harry and I stormed the dorm and asked who was creating the disturbance? Like I said, *Eastern* was a no-nonsense camp created to teach the qualities that it takes to become a great basketball player, including *discipline*.

The players sensed they had crossed a line, so nobody was ready to confess when we questioned them. No problem—we got all forty of the campers out of the dorm and took them outside for a half hour of late-night exercises. After the workout, the campers stood at attention for fifteen minutes with the mosquitoes biting at their tired, sweaty bodies—besides a great basketball experience, the camp was also known for its mosquitoes, and they were as thick as fog that night. But not one of those campers dared to make a move or complain.

Scratching from the aerial assault and still dripping with sweat, the boys were sent back to their sleeping bags and not another sound was heard from them. That was *Eastern Ohio Basketball Camp*—all basketball, all discipline, no-nonsense. It was there that I got to really know what made the Huggins family so successful in the game of basketball, and becoming friends with them would essentially shape my life and the path of my own coaching career.

When I met him, Bob Huggins was a part-time assistant coach at Ohio State, and he was really anxious to get head-coaching experience—even if it meant stepping away from the 'big time' for a while. I always gave Bob credit for that because he had a pretty nice deal at Ohio State. He could've gotten other major college assistant jobs and methodically advanced along that path without ever experiencing life at the lower college level. But choosing the more patient, passive path wasn't—how shall I say this—the *Bob Huggins* way.

I was actually sitting beside Bob at *Eastern Ohio Camp* when the pay phone rang with a call that would change his life—*and mine*. When he came back to the table, he told me that he had just taken the head-coaching job at *Walsh College*, a small *NAIA* basketball program in North Canton, Ohio. After he informed me he had accepted the Walsh job, Bob said these magic words to me: *Do you want to come with me?*

I was twenty-five years old and intoxicated by the thought of putting my basketball energy into a *Huggins* coaching project, so I jumped at the opportunity. Almost thirty years later, I'm certain it was the best decision I could have possibly made at that point in my career.

I learned so much during the three years I spent with Bob Huggins at *Walsh College*. We had a great staff: Dan Peters, who went on to become a head Division-I college coach at *Youngstown State*; Steve Burgess, who was a sports marketing wiz; and me. We worked our tails off and had a blast doing it. We tried everything from painting Walsh basketball logos on barns to establishing the nicest small-college press guide in the country. We were at Walsh, but to Bob Huggins, Dan Peters, Scott Burgess and me, we might as well have been at *UCLA*.

Bob once told me on a recruiting trip to Canada that he was sure he would win a national championship at the major college level someday. Bob wasn't cocky; he simply had a vision and he was constantly preparing to fulfill that vision. It was Bob's big visions that pushed us to treat *Walsh College* as if it *were UCLA*.

With Bob's contacts and our staff work ethic, we went from 14-16 the first season, to 23-8 in our second season, to 34-0 in our third and final year at Walsh—1983. We lost that year in Kansas City in the *NAIA National Tournament*.

After the 1983 season at Walsh, Bob really wanted to move on and get a major college job. He had interviewed for the *Youngstown State* job and finished second in 1982, and he was very anxious to get back on that level. Feeling like he had gained the head-coaching experience he needed to put on his resume, he decided to make a strategic career move and go to Central Florida as a top assistant for Chuck Machock.

Although going to Central Florida was a risk, Bob felt he had a better chance to get a Division-I head-coaching job if he were coaching at that level. Bob was correct—and as I have already explained, and most basketball people know—things have worked out pretty well for Bob Huggins in the coaching profession.

Besides the fact that Bob Huggins has been a dear friend and mentor to me, I tell this story because his leaving Walsh to become an assistant at Central Florida required *me* to make a move. I wasn't sure what I would do for several days, then Bob advised me to get head-coaching experience somewhere—just as he had done at Walsh. He told me that I should get it on my resume that I am capable of being a head coach and he suggested that someday we might be able to get back together on a staff someplace.

With Bob's advice in mind, I actually interviewed for the head-coaching job at *Thiel College*, a small *NCAA Division-III* school in Pennsylvania, and I finished second for the position. I really wanted the Thiel job, and I believed that being with Bob Huggins at Walsh made me a perfect fit there. When Thiel didn't hire me, I found another thing Coach Huggins had told me to be true: *A coach really needs to get lucky securing his first job and then he has to make his own breaks the rest of the way.* With that, I decided to try my luck at finding a job as a head coach at the high school level.

The search for a good high school job landed me an interview at a mid-sized school near Wooster, Ohio, called Triway. I received my interview at Triway High School because the administration there was looking for a *Charlie Huggins disciple*—a title I was proud to accept.

I went to my Triway interview and decided to throw the whole shooting match at them. I brought bumper stickers that said: "Triway STATE CHAMPS!" I took schedule cards and a detailed playbook complete with my written philosophy on everything involved in building a program; I used everything I had learned from all of the great coaches I had known and studied. I wore a three-piece suit and pretended Triway was *UCLA*, because—in my mind—it may as well have been UCLA!

The administration offered me the Triway job and I accepted with the idea that it would be a nice way to get a *couple years'* experience running a program so that I could get back to the college level.

Well, a couple years turned into nineteen—and almost two decades later I was still there, enjoying every second of implementing many of the ideas I will share here in these pages.

All these years later, I remain close friends with Bob Huggins, Dan Peters and Steve Burgess. Bob Huggins has often told me that the Walsh College years were possibly the most enjoyable years of his coaching life; in many ways, I agree with him. We were all in our mid-twenties, and we tried everything. Some things worked, some didn't, but I can honestly say the time I spent on Bob Huggins' staff were the three most formative years of my career as they relate to the coaching and program-building methods I have implemented at Triway and Hoover.

Looking back, Bob Huggins played a huge role in getting me started in my career as a head coach, but he wasn't my only influence; I received helpful advice from a number of highly successful coaches. Another of those coaches, Dan Peters, once said to me, *"The big time is wherever a coach is happy"*—and I believe his quote to be so very true. Most coaches set out with some career goals to get to a certain level—and there's nothing wrong with that. But to achieve ultimate goals, coaches must always put heart and soul into the job they have right now.

When I interviewed at Triway back in the early 1980's—even though I thought I would go there for just a couple years to gain some experience as a head coach before heading back to the college level—I built my program as though I would be there forever. Almost two decades later, nineteen years from the day I accepted the Triway job, I was still at Triway.

Many of my friends and colleagues wondered why I never left Triway during those nineteen years to take on *big-time jobs* when I was offered opportunities. The question I always asked in response was this: What is a *big- time job?* When this question was greeted with silence, I asked the following series of questions:

Is the big time winning *twelve* straight conference championships? Is the *big time* earning *two* State of Ohio *AP* Poll Championships? Is it playing in big games in front of full houses night in and night out, year in and year out? Does the *big time* mean winning *seven* District Championships? Is the *big time* earning *two* trips to the *Final Four?*

Looking back at the journey, I'd say that coaching at Triway *was*, in fact, *a big-time coaching job*, and after hearing me ask those questions, most people agree.

I had a blast running my basketball program at Triway High School for the time I was there. I coached many young men and met many people at Triway that I consider life-long friends. When I left Triway after nineteen wonderful years, I didn't leave because North Canton Hoover was a *better* place than Triway; I left because it was time for a *new* challenge.

Heck, all I really ever wanted as a head coach was to have a program like the one I watched and played in at Salem High School back in the 1970's. So I put my heart and soul into my programs at Triway and Hoover because that's what I learned to do while growing up in the Salem Basketball Program—and because that's what Bob Huggins taught me to do in the time I spent with him.

100 (Kramer)

Whether it was the idea of a higher power or simply something in the stars, I believe the plan for me—starting the day I was born—was always for me to become a head basketball coach. I earned reasonably good grades in school, so I had options when it came to choosing a career path, but every path I explored led back to what was firmly embedded in my DNA—coaching basketball.

How young was I when *I* became aware of the plan? Here's a quick story my mom still loves to tell that indicates I was pretty young:

One day when I was a shade younger than four years old, my mom walked into my playroom—a wonderland of toys that would have made Toys 'R Us *jealous—to check on me. She was worried—as she tells it—because I had been unusually quiet, and a quiet room usually meant I had found trouble. When she entered the room, she saw me sitting on the floor playing with some old burnt-out Christmas tree light bulbs. There were ten of them—five red and five green. When she asked me what I was doing, I told her that they were my basketball people, and I was coaching them.*

Now, coaching those light bulbs was more of a sign that I idolized *Dan Kramer*—my dad, my hero, and the coach I grew up watching—more than it was a sign that I was a basketball coach's version of *Mozart*, orchestrating my own team before the age of five. However, the story does show that the seeds to my career in coaching were sewn at a very young age. From that point, my path to becoming a head coach was quite a bit from the one taken by Coach Montgomery.

For every Randy Montgomery—a distinctly qualified coach from the *Huggins basketball tree*—there are a far greater number of guys like me who have really had to work their way through the lower levels of programs to get their first shot. In other words, the name of the road I traveled was *perseverance*—a route that might serve as an inspiration to young coaches who are starting from step one down a path that they want to lead to a head-coaching position.

I began my coaching career when my playing career as an *NCAA Division-III* college basketball player ended due to a ruptured disc and stress fracture to the fifth lumbar vertebrae in my lower back. I incurred the injury during a preseason workout at *Mount Union College* where I had transferred after playing two seasons for one of the nation's finest collegiate coaches at any level, *Steve Moore*, at *The College of Wooster*. Whereas it *was* very difficult to walk away from my playing career because I had become a *competent* player at Wooster, suffice it to say that basketball fans around the world didn't take even a fraction of a second to mourn.

Truth be told, the back injury was a blessing in disguise, because it allowed me to get a jump on my coaching career a couple of years before I would graduate from college. This was important for me because—like most young coaches—I did not have a surefire path paved to becoming a head coach.

My dad was a very good head coach in his time at *Akron Hoban High School* in the late 1970's and early 1980's. He coached some pretty good teams and some very solid high school athletes—most notably a player by the name of *Butch Reynolds* who would go on to fame and fortune in the world of track and field by winning an Olympic gold medal and establishing a world 400-meter record that would stand for the better part of a decade.

Whereas I idolized my dad's players—like Butch Reynolds—and my dad was obviously the number one influence on my career choice, it had been almost a decade since he last coached a game when I began my job search. Therefore, my ties to any coaching tree were limited.

I believe that this part of my story is relevant to most young people who aspire to become head coaches, because most coaches *do* start out relatively unknown and have to hustle their way up the coaching ladder. I had no connection to *a Bob Huggins* who would make my resume impossible to ignore, and—whereas it was something that I remember fondly—my playing career wasn't the type of career that gave my name instant credibility as a coach. With all of this in mind, I knew I was going to have to hustle if I was ever to make it in the coaching profession.

While still working toward my degree at Mount Union, I hit the trail and was fortunate enough to land my first coaching job when I joined Coach Tom Brabson's staff at Alliance High School. Coach Brabson was a well-respected coach who had played his high school ball at *Barberton High School* for legendary coach *Jack Greynolds.* Coach Greynolds' son Jackie was also on Coach Brabson's staff as Alliance's junior varsity coach, so I had joined two coaches with impeccable coaching pedigrees—a very important step for me early in my career.

I worked under Coach Brabson for two years at Alliance, a small city school district with a distinct inner-city feel. My first year I served as the eighth grade coach at Stanton Middle School and my second year as the freshmen coach at Alliance High School. Those were two great years of experience, and I am more thankful to Tom Brabson than even *he* knows. Tom worked with me to implement a system of play, took me on trips to coaching clinics, and generally treated me like a colleague and friend. I loved working for Tom Brabson during those two years, and I wanted to stay in Alliance once I earned my teaching certificate.

Unfortunately, when I graduated from Mount Union College in 1992, Alliance had no teaching positions available. So, with no source of steady income, I returned home to live with my parents in Cuyahoga Falls, Ohio—where I signed up to be a substitute teacher at every local school district in the Akron area. Subbing wasn't what I wanted to do, but I figured it was better than nothing, and I hoped it would help me land a coaching job. Sure enough, in the fall of 1992, I was lucky enough to find a spot on the staff of another legendary Ohio high school coach.

This time the coaching job was at *Cuyahoga Falls High School* under Head Coach *Mike Meneer.* In 1992, Coach Meneer would be in his first year as the coach at Cuyahoga Falls after winning a state championship in the early 1980's at *Akron Central Hower* and guiding Akron St. Vincent Mary to a couple of *"Sweet-16"* appearances in the early 1990's. Coach Meneer was at the end of his teaching career, and he took the Cuyahoga Falls job because it was his hometown and his alma mater, and that's where he wanted to finish his coaching career.

Although I needed money to pay my bills and Coach Meneer didn't have a paid position available, I joined his staff anyway—as an *unpaid* assistant. I knew that working under another *coaching great* would be a terrific learning experience, and it would give me a branch on another coaching tree that would improve my resume and continue to allow me to push toward becoming a head coach.

Looking back, I learned different things under Coach Meneer than I did under Coach Brabson at Alliance, but it was, in fact, another great learning experience. Coach Meneer was very good at working with his players, but his gift, at least from my standpoint, was that he was the best coach for whom I ever worked when it came to public relations.

When Mike Meneer walked into a room, he immediately gained control of it. People were drawn to him, and that allowed him to be a great leader in the community that transcended the boundaries of his basketball program.

Coach Meneer had an uncanny knack for making anyone who was interested in the basketball program feel like he or she was a part of it, yet he did that without allowing too many people into the inner circle of the program. That's a tough balance to keep, and Mike was a magician when it came to doing it. What was the formula? Well, one part was Mike's substantial God-given charisma; the other part didn't take any God-given gift—he simply treated everyone well.

I don't think it's possible to overestimate the importance of being a positive figure in the community. Coaching at a public high school means there are going to be down years, and a coach with a positive image who is liked by a majority of the community has a far better chance of weathering difficult times than one who is abrasive. Mike Meneer was loved because he treated people well, and people wanted to be around Mike Meneer and his basketball program.

I don't mean to paint a picture of a coach who was without his detractors, because after spending over a decade as a head coach I know that there is no such thing, regardless of wins and championships. There is simply a faction of every community that wakes up in the morning and looks for negativity, and a coach who works in the public eye is a natural target for those people. The major lesson I took from working with Coach Meneer the one year I was on his staff as a volunteer assistant is this: By treating people well and expanding his list of allies, a coach not only decreases the number of his detractors, but he also eliminates most of any audience that may otherwise listen to the remaining detractors when they complain.

Admittedly, early in my career as a head coach, I lost sight of that lesson, and it was almost disastrous. Since then I have worked hard at the public relations part of the job I learned from Mike Meneer and honestly, I have found the job to be far more enjoyable when I have had an enthusiastic and supportive community to share it with.

I loved working for Mike Meneer, and I truly thought that spending a year on his staff as a volunteer assistant while substituting in the *Cuyahoga Falls City School District* would lead to a full-time teaching position. Unfortunately, sometimes *the best-laid plans* don't work out perfectly.

Despite the strong connections I made with Mike Meneer and the others on his staff, I was frustrated to find out that there were no teaching positions available in Cuyahoga Falls on a full-time basis. So, whereas I would have loved to stay on Coach Meneer's staff and volunteer another year to gain more coaching experience, it was time for me to adapt and alter *the plan* so I could start making a living. Ironically, the solution to my job search was in the hallway in the very school where I couldn't get full-time work.

Former Cuyahoga Falls Head Coach Henry Cobb, the man Mike Meneer had replaced a year earlier, was still teaching in the building when he entered the running for the job to become the head basketball coach at *Canton South High School*, a *Division-II* school about forty minutes south down *Route* 77 in Canton, Ohio. Coach Cobb had been my brother Steve's head coach in 1991 at Cuyahoga Falls for a team that spent a good part of the 1990-91 season ranked in the top three of the state's *AP Division-I Poll*. That team featured two players who would go on to have good careers at the *NCAA Division-I* college level—seven-footer *Robbie Eggers* who went on to play for *Coach Bob Knight* at *Indiana*, and *Landon Hackim* who went on to have a great career at *Miami of Ohio*.

I was coaching in Alliance the year my brother played for Henry Cobb, but I used to slip unnoticed into the upper deck in Cuyahoga Falls' vast gymnasium and watch Coach Cobb conduct practice when my schedule allowed me to do so—something I would strongly urge coaches of all ages to do.

I was always impressed with the discipline and organization Henry Cobb put into his practices, and those practices really paid off during the 1990-91 season. I watched my brother Steve—the point guard for that team—and his teammates dismantle most of their opponents on the way to a twenty-win campaign. Watching Coach Cobb's practices, then seeing how they helped his team transform into a *winning machine* on game nights, made me wish I could work with him. So, on a Monday in mid-May of 1993, when he approached me in the hallway at

Cuyahoga Falls High School and asked me if I would be interested in going with him to Canton South if he were to get the job, I jumped and told him that was *exactly* what I wanted to do—*if* I could get a full-time teaching job.

That same evening Henry Cobb was offered the job at Canton South and accepted it. The next day, he told me that the administration at South was going to allow him to bring an assistant with him, but that the assistant would have to interview for the teaching position that was available. Coach Cobb stressed to me that the district was going to require the candidate to be someone who—first and foremost—would bring enthusiasm to the classroom. In other words, they weren't going to pay someone to teach just because the new head basketball coach needed an assistant.

Although I knew little about the Canton Local School District and Canton South High School, other than it had a *decent* basketball tradition, I knew that going there with Henry Cobb was the big break I needed to start my teaching career and really become serious about establishing myself as a head-coaching candidate.

As I figured he would, Coach Cobb made good on his promise to procure an interview for me. So in late May of 1993, I went to the district's middle school, *Faircrest Memorial Middle School*, knowing that it would be up to me to secure my first teaching job by selling myself as the type of professional who would work tirelessly in the classroom.

To any aspiring young coach, this bit of advice might be the most important advice one could ever hear: Don't go into coaching unless you *also* love to teach in the classroom. Without a doubt, my love of teaching sprang from working with kids on the athletic field. When I was a teenager and in high school, I did volunteer work coaching for our local *Little League Baseball Association* in Cuyahoga Falls. It was those early experiences with coaching that allowed me to find joy in working with young people, and the joy that I found in those early experiences, coupled with wanting to be a basketball coach, led me to pursue a career in education.

That said, had I gone into the classroom and found the experience to be unfulfilling, I would have never pursued this line of work any further. A public school high school basketball coach spends well over half of most days in the classroom as a teacher—what a disservice it would be to a school district for a candidate to accept a teaching job knowing all he really wanted to do was coach. My student-teaching experiences and my experience with substitute teaching made it easy for me to go into that interview at the middle school and sell the idea that I had a strong desire to be a great teacher, because—the fact of the matter is—I did.

Looking back and knowing all the things I have learned over the course of my many years of experience in the classroom, I doubt my responses in that first teaching interview at Faircrest were all that impressive. As I'm sure is the case in most professions, experience is the greatest teacher, and mine was limited. But I was hungry for that job, and my guess is that what my answers lacked in knowledge I made up for with my palpable enthusiasm for the opportunity. So a few days later, Mr. Tim Welker—perhaps the finest *leader* for whom I have ever worked—called me and offered me the opportunity to become his seventh-grade language arts teacher, a job I eagerly accepted.

Teaching in the classroom is obviously different in many ways from coaching in the gym, but at the root of both is a responsibility to *lead* young people, and I immediately took the responsibility to lead in the classroom as seriously as I had always taken the responsibility to lead on the basketball court. I was teaching seventh-graders in the classroom and—although some people find that stage of adolescence to be obnoxious—I found the perspective of the average seventh-grader to be a perfect diversion from the stresses that the coaching world had to offer. I mean, seventh graders don't know what they are—children or young adults—so they are still very impressionable and teachable while providing just enough naïve humor to keep the job entertaining and loose at all times. My job was perfect *for me* at Faircrest Middle School— great building, great principal, and colleagues who would become my friends. I loved teaching in the *Canton Local School System*.

Likewise, the coaching was *exactly* what I had hoped it would be when I decided to follow Henry Cobb to Canton South. I was the junior varsity coach and the program had a very strong sophomore class. In fact, after spending a summer with our new players at South, I felt there was pretty good talent from the senior class on down through the middle school—an assessment that played out as being correct over the course of the next several years and Henry Cobb led the program to tremendous success on the court.

At this point I want to stress that I am grateful to every head coach who mentored me in my early years. But besides my father, Henry Cobb was *the* person I have to thank most for getting my first shot as a head coach. When I started with him, I was a twenty-three-year-old kid, and I *thought* I knew a lot more than I *actually* knew. This can be a good thing and a bad thing.

Regardless of what anyone wants to admit, it takes someone with extreme confidence in his knowledge and teaching ability to walk into a locker room of teenage athletes and command the group's respect, and if that confidence is not supreme at the outset, the group will detect uncertainty, as individuals will tend to challenge the philosophy being implemented. I never had that problem, because I was always confident in my leadership ability.

However, that confidence can cut both ways, because it grew out of the idea in my mind that I was ready to be a head coach before I ever coached *a junior varsity game*—and *that* thought was misguided. Henry Cobb was the man there to nurture me through my early years as an upper-level assistant. He was there to tell me when I was doing a good job, and like my father would have done had he been the head coach, Henry was there to let me know when something I had done was unacceptable. Honestly, had it not been for Henry Cobb overseeing my everyday work, I may have never developed into head-coaching material.

The biggest reason I felt I was fast-tracked to become a head coach before my thirtieth birthday was because my junior varsity teams were winning a great percentage of their games. Fifteen, sixteen and seventeen-win seasons became the norm in my six years as the junior varsity coach, and winning—as I have come to say—is one of the biggest liars in sports.

See, when a coach wins games, especially a young one, he tends to think that everything he does is on point, and nothing could be further from the truth. As a matter of fact, I'll tell in a later section why I believe that the *worst* seasons record-wise that I ever experienced as a head coach were the ones that helped me the most to reach my potential. At South, my junior varsity teams were winning, the varsity team was winning, and from where I sat, it looked like that was all that mattered.

But Henry was there to show me the importance of things beyond winning. He showed me the meaning of approaching the practice floor like it is the most important part of the job—because it is; also, he allowed me to see how he dealt with the inner-workings of running a basketball program—from fund-raising, to improving facilities, to public relations. I am grateful for everything Henry Cobb did for me, but most of all, I am grateful that he trusted me enough to let me coach and put some of my ideas into our system at South.

Sounds simple enough, but some head coaches don't like to delegate too much responsibility to assistants. The longer I worked with Henry Cobb, the more responsibility he gave me, and the more freedom he allowed me to have with using some of my own ideas to supplement his system. We made a good team.

Henry was a great defensive coach with a knack for running a tight and disciplined ship; on the flip side, I was the guy that had to come up with ways to crack his defenses in practice so that my junior varsity players could get decent shots and challenge the varsity. As a head coach, I have been labeled as offensive-minded, and this is the way it happened. Had I not been creative on the offensive side of the ball as a junior varsity coach at Canton South, my sophomores and freshmen would *never* have gotten a shot off against a Henry Cobb-coached varsity defense in practice. (More on this later.)

After a while, some of the things I was using in practice against Henry's defenses became part of our program's offensive system, and before I knew it, I was acting as associate offensive-coordinator to Henry at the varsity level. I say *associate* because I don't want anyone to think I was in full charge of the offense. Make no mistake, we were running Henry's base system, but he was allowing me to make adjustments and implement sets for use in the flow of the game. Simply put, he allowed me to develop as a coach.

My final season on Henry Cobb's staff at Canton South was the 1999-2000 season. During the summer of 1999, Henry decided that he would like me to move up to the varsity assistant position, a move he had asked me if I was interested in making before, but one I had declined for two reasons: first, because I felt like I needed experience running my own bench; second, because I felt Henry's assistants in the past had been more about doing administrative things off the floor—paperwork guys, so to speak—and I wanted to coach.

However, having six years of bench experience in hand at the junior varsity level, and knowing that Coach Cobb had shown more and more trust in my *X's & O's*, I thought my next logical step would be to move up and work exclusively at the top level of the program for the 1999-2000 season.

As it turned out, it was a great move. That season we returned almost none of the kids we had relied heavily upon the previous season in winning twenty games and finishing runners-up to Coach Montgomery's Triway Titans in the *Canton D-II District*. We did, however, return our super sophomore shooting guard, Jerry Prestier.

Jerry is still today the most accurate three-point shooter I have ever seen, and his lightning quick release—a skill he honed in his driveway, oftentimes with his mom rebounding—almost comically struck fear in the hearts of opposing defenses as his freshman season at the varsity level wore on. I say *comically*, because our offense during the 1998-99 season was actually built around two imposing physical specimens—6'10" 260-pound Roy Geer, and 6'7", 270-pound Andre Batiste. Next to those two, Jerry's 5'11", 130-pound, middle school physique made him an afterthought for most defenses early in the season—that is until opposing coaches realized that while Roy and Andre were wearing them down with body blows on the inside, Jerry was landing undefended haymakers from behind the three-point arc.

As the season wore on in 1998-99, teams were very likely to face a guard, our little ninth-grader Jerry Prestier, on the perimeter, and collapse the rest of the defense around our two 'bigs' on the inside. That tactic did slow Jerry's scoring down because, as a ninth-grader, the other aspects of his offensive game were limited. But it also prepared him for the way teams would guard him for the rest of his career; it also really loosened up the defense on the inside for Roy and Andre to go to work—thus the twenty wins in 1999.

Returning with Jerry Prestier for the 1999-2000 season were several players who had created the supporting cast on the great team of the previous season, several of whom had some upside in taking on greater roles—including a couple very capable scorers in wingmen Josh Doll and Tony Milini. These two players—and some of their teammates—had experienced some shining moments along the way, but would need to step up and provide consistent tangibles if we were to continue our run of success at Canton South.

Rounding out the 1999-2000 roster would be two sensational incoming ninth-graders who would cut their teeth at the varsity level and eventually lead Coach Cobb to a *Final Four* three years later—only to lose to LeBron James and St. Vincent-St. Mary. Ronnie Bourquin and Jeremy Richards both ended up being All-Ohio basketball players in their senior season, but they also gave us some great moments and solid play in their freshmen season. As I said, it was an interesting mix of players, albeit a group that nobody really knew anything about.

The experience as the varsity assistant that year was a fantastic one for me, and the opportunity to help game plan and test my concepts at the varsity level was invaluable. The more the year wore on, the more teams threw 'junk' defenses at us to keep Jerry from getting open looks at the basket, so coaching the offense and keeping our best shooter involved meant making one adjustment after another, and Coach Cobb let me do it just like I had done our first six years together when trying to get my junior varsity players shots against his defenses in practice.

In the end, that team did not win a league or district title, but it played in one hotly contested game after another against the best competition the area had to offer. It was a team that overachieved on many levels and inspired those who watched it on a nightly basis. Looking back, it was working with those kids of which so little was expected during that 1999-2000 season that really re-wet my appetite for running my own program.

Feeling as though I was more ready than ever to take over a head-coaching position, I was excited in late April of 2000 when Fairless High School—a school district that bordered Canton Local—had an opening for a new head boys' basketball coach. Whereas Fairless didn't have great teams every year, I knew from scouting and coaching against Fairless that the program did have some years where it made some nice runs. So, I thought the job was perfect for me.

Making things even more perfect, the principal at Fairless was a man by the name of Richard Hull—the same man who had been the principal at *Stanton Middle School* in Alliance during my time as a student teacher and eighth-grade coach in the Alliance basketball program. Mr. Hull was—and still is—a man I deeply respect, and I will always be very appreciative of the time he spent mentoring me in my early days while I was trying to get started in the field. I wanted the Fairless job more than I had ever wanted anything else in my career, and I felt I had a great shot at getting it.

In early August of 2000, after several twists and turns—and a decade of being singularly focused on my goal of running a program— I was named the new head basketball coach at Fairless High School. Just as was the case when I became Coach Cobb's junior varsity coach at Canton South, I felt I was more than qualified and as ready as I'd ever be to start leading my own program—a confident thought, and one I would find to be true on some levels, and not so much on others.

3

The Interview:
Selling a grand vision

500

MY FIRST CHANCE to sell my vision—my *best-laid plans* for leading a public high school basketball program—came at Triway in the spring of 1983. I took posters, bumper stickers and schedule cards, along with a complete packet outlining plans for the program. I took all of those things to my interview at Triway because I felt then—and still do today—that marketing is a big factor in selling my vision to an interviewing committee. Once that's done, of course, a coach *must* win!

Knowing winning would be important, even though Triway had experienced seven straight sub-par seasons, I talked in my interview about making it to *The Final Four* in Columbus. I told the people interviewing me at Triway that if it wasn't what they were striving for, then they should *not* hire me. I also told them that I felt all I needed was *their* support to allow me to lead, and we would turn Triway into a basketball power.

My sales pitch worked—because it was *sincere*—and I was awarded the job over fifty applicants. Once on the job, I immediately began testing the administration's willingness to provide the backing it *claimed* it would give me during the interview.

I started by approaching my athletic director about scheduling Youngstown Rayen—the reigning state champion in what was then called *Class-AA* in the State of Ohio. Rayen was absolutely *the* power in the 1980's, winning twelve straight district championships—which in Ohio earn a trip to the "*Sweet-16*"—and making multiple trips to Columbus for the *Final Four*.

My athletic director thought I was crazy because, besides the fact that Rayen was perhaps the best *AA* program in Ohio, it was also an hour and a half bus ride from rural Triway to inner-city Youngstown. But I knew that if we were ever to be the best, we would need to see the best up close, so I continued to full-court pressure my bosses until they finally succumbed and granted my wish—a home and home with Youngstown Rayen.

In my first year as a head coach, we headed to Youngstown and took a charter bus of fans with us. Of course inner-city Youngstown is quite a bit different than rural Triway, so the looks on the faces of my players when we pulled into Rayen was one of frightened curiosity. Unfortunately, we played with those looks on our faces and lost by forty points.

We rode home that night—a bus ride of well over an hour long—and when we got off the bus, we went straight into our gym *and practiced*. Now, understand that I fully *expected* the beating we took, but I wanted to instill in my players that it was *not* acceptable. Everyone—and I do mean everyone—thought I was certifiably bonkers, but we began to improve after that and *believe* in the *unthinkable* goals that I had put in front of the program.

The next season Rayen had to come to Triway to return the date. Everyone, including the Rayen players and coaches, thought it would be another thirty or forty point blowout. After all, Rayen had gone on to win the *Ohio Class-AA State Championship* the previous year, and their program returned plenty of talent from that team.

In the spirit of sportsmanship—or perhaps gamesmanship—I decided we would kick the night off by taking the opportunity to honor The State Champs before the game with a cake and short ceremony. The Rayen players and coaches seemed to enjoy the celebration, and their jovial approach to pre-game lingered into the early stages of play, which helped keep the game close and build our confidence that we could compete with them.

We had a *decent* team that second year, and the longer we continued to compete, the more the players and the crowd started to believe something special was happening in the Triway gym. The game went down to the wire, and, to make a long story short, we beat Rayen that night by three points. Then *we* celebrated like *we* had just won the state title!

After the game, Rayen was not nearly as jovial. In fact, they threw the cake on the floor and left angry. But Rayen's anger signaled that the Triway Titan program had arrived. In my opinion, that game turned the whole program around, and at that point the entire administration was *100%* behind the plan that I had sold in my interview.

Now, it may seem like I was off on a tangent down memory lane there, but the connection to the interview is simple: creating *the best-laid plans* and talking about it in the interview is absolutely critical. In 1983, at Triway—before I had ever coached a varsity basketball game—I talked about competing for the state title. The plan started with going out and playing *the best* competition I could find.

Playing the best seemed outlandish for a Triway program that had experienced seven losing seasons in a row prior to my tenure there, but the administration got excited in the interview, and I kept referring back to that interview every time I went to them with something new and innovative. It started with my administration supporting me and allowing me to schedule Youngstown Rayen.

Of course, I didn't know that we would beat Rayen, but I was certain that we would be able to compete with them a little bit better the second time, because the fear factor would be eliminated and the game would be on our home court. When we won that game, it all became real, and 'The Pit'—the name affectionately given to our gym at Triway—was born.

After that, each time I approached the administration and something seemed like a hair-brained idea, I reminded them that they promised me support in my approach to leading the Triway program—and I reminded them of the Rayen victory. From there on, most of my ideas didn't seem so far-fetched.

There were other things I sold in the interview at Triway that dealt with marketing the program and making it a piece of the community, and the way that played out evolved over a period of time. At one point, we had a 3-on-3 tournament at Triway with 500 competitors. We got a car dealer to sponsor the event for $10,000. The tournament was a huge weekend basketball extravaganza complete with a circus tent, hot-air balloons and celebrities giving basketball clinics. Men named Dale Currana and Bob Maruna helped me run it, and it evolved into a major event in Wayne County each August, complete with billboards and full-page newspaper coverage from several papers.

I'm not suggesting every coach walk into an interview and talk about running a 3-on-3 tournament. However, ideas like this show a vision of *the best-laid plans* in an interview and it is that vision that gets people excited. The vision a coach sells, I feel, is the most important thing he can do when trying to acquire a new job. Much of this I learned from Bob Huggins, as he allowed me to watch and learn while he sold *his* vision.

Bob nearly got the *Youngstown State* job after just two years at *Walsh College*, and I'm convinced he came so close so early in his career because he was the master at selling his vision—which in his case was winning a *National Championship* at a school like Youngstown State or *Akron*. Two years later, Bob Huggins did get the Akron job and although he didn't win a *National Championship* there, he did get the *Zips* into their first ever *NCAA Tournament*.

That year, 1986, Akron played its *Youngstown Rayen* in the first round of the NCAA's when Coach Huggins' Zips took on a Gary Grant led Michigan team that had been ranked in the top five in the country most of the season. Akron led Michigan for the first thirty-five minutes of the game before running out of steam and losing a close game down the stretch. However, even though his team lost that day, Bob Huggins' vision was on display for the whole country to see, and that led to his accepting the job at the University of Cincinnati where he eventually made a *Final Four*.

Of course Coach Huggins has since taken his hall-of-fame credentials to his alma mater, West Virginia University, where he took *the Mountaineers* to a *Final Four* in just his third season as the head coach. Bob Huggins will be mentioned throughout this book, because he is a great friend and a coach who has made a huge impact on my career, starting with the grand visions he taught me to have for *my* program.

Having that vision has always stuck with me. Whether a coach is interviewing at Triway, Hoover, Akron or West Virginia, I believe it's all about selling a vision of *the best-laid plans* that will lead to greatness. I witnessed Bob Huggins doing this as he built his career; it's what I have tried to do in every interview I've ever been in; and it's what I'd suggest any coach prepare to do prior to interviewing.

100 (Kramer)

My first bit of advice to any coach going into an interview is to make sure he *chooses* his attitude just as carefully as he chooses which tie to wear with his favorite shirt. Attitude is a choice, and the first thing the committee is going to notice—after that sharp tie—is the candidate's enthusiasm for the chance to interview.

Here's the way I look at it: interviewing is a chance for me to sit in front of a captive audience and talk about one of my favorite subjects—

the passion I have for leading a basketball program using *my best-laid plans*. To me, that sounds like fun.

Prior to receiving my first position as a head coach at Fairless, I was afforded a number of interviews. Several of those early interviews I entered knowing a couple variables were stacked against me that dictated I would be a long shot to get the job. First off, most schools with good basketball traditions give a huge edge to coaches with head-coaching experience, and I had none. The second major variable is that oftentimes a school has a clear-cut favorite for its job before the interviewing ever starts.

These things may seem unfair, but they are what they are. I know some coaches that won't accept an interview if the odds are stacked against them. I say go anyway—especially if it's a coach with no head-coaching experience. Two reasons: first, like anything else, the more a coach gains experience with interviews, the better he or she becomes at the process; second, administrators network just like coaches do—which means finishing second in one interview may very well make a coach a stronger candidate for the next position that opens.

I interviewed at three schools before I was offered my first head-coaching position, and I knew I wasn't a favorite going into any of them. In each of those first three situations, I made it to a second interview and was one of the final two candidates. Each time I went in with the disadvantage of having no experience as a head coach, but I enjoyed each experience and learned many things from each.

Those experiences were invaluable to me in eventually making my name one that *would* be considered a top candidate for open positions. Two things propelled me into the final two at those first three interviews: my enthusiasm for the chance to interview and the fact that I was prepared with some items that made my vision tangible to the committee.

Coach Montgomery wrote about having bumper stickers and t-shirts that said: *"Triway State Champs"* when he went into his first interview. I love his ideas and did some similar things along those lines. However, I also had one other very important item to hand to each member of the committee upon entering the interview: *my coaching portfolio*—a document I began writing when I was in my first year of coaching as a twenty-year-old middle school coach at Stanton Middle School in Alliance.

Before each interview, I take my portfolio to a local print shop and have it professionally bound with a cover that displays a picture of the school's mascot and school name where I will be interviewing. I pay for enough copies for each member of the committee to have one to keep, and I always have a couple extra printed just in case.

The first thing I do when walking into the interview is pass the portfolios out and use them to segue into introducing myself. I use this approach to seize control of the room. Of course there are questions that will come from the committee, and I enjoy answering those questions. But by the time I am done introducing myself to the room, I want to make sure I have already set myself apart from the other candidates; my portfolio allows me to establish myself as a leader before any questions are ever asked.

I never expect members of the interviewing committee to read every page—after years of revisions and additions, my portfolio had become a lengthy document. Regardless, it showed a level of drive and preparation that set me apart from the average candidate with *no* head-coaching experience and it was also a way of leveling the playing field with candidates who *did* have experience as a head coach—which brings me to my second piece of interviewing advice to every aspiring head coach:

Start your portfolio *right now*. Looking back, it *is* a lot of work; however, written a little bit at a time, it fits right in with the learning process that goes with progressing up through the coaching ranks. Beyond being a great tool to help sell an interview, it is also an invaluable way to self-assess and reflect on the way a philosophy is evolving with experience. I still have my portfolio today, and I still add to it and revise it from time to time. In fact, much of that portfolio has led to the text written in these pages. All in all, the portfolio has been a very useful tool for me over the years.

From there, like Coach Montgomery, I believe the interview is a sales pitch—an opportunity for a coach to sell his vision of greatness for a program to the people who will be making the hire. When Randy Montgomery went into his first interview, he held the upper hand in that he was on the staff of Bob Huggins at Walsh College, and he had a definite branch on the Huggins family coaching tree. When he went into his interview, he sold his vision for running a program and the choice was a no-brainer for Triway. The rest is history.

As I sought my first job as a head coach, I didn't have the '*Huggins thing*' going for me. I had worked for a number of excellent high school head coaches, but none of that was going to make me the primary candidate for most jobs, so I took a much different route to the head-coaching ranks than Coach Montgomery.

I think the moral of the story in this section is this: A coach who has *a Bob Huggins* on his resume is very fortunate and *should* be considered a desirable candidate before he ever walks in the door to interview. Coaches who don't have that type of advantage need to find another way to show a readiness for the challenges of running a basketball program—like the portfolio I used to show those who interviewed me that I had put years of thought into creating my idea of *the best-laid plans* for leading a program.

Either way, the tangible *things* a coach takes to the interview only get him so far. In the end, it's a coach's ability to walk in the room once he has the opportunity to interview and sell his vision with enthusiasm and passion that leads to that first opportunity to be a head coach. Of course, once the job is offered, the next part is just as important as the interview: a coach's decision whether or not to accept the job.

4

Choosing a Head Coaching Job:

The most important job in the nation or—
a gateway to getting fired

500 (Montgomery)

AFTER ALL MY years in coaching, I have learned *this* about finding the perfect job: I don't feel that a coach should ever go into a job looking for his next one. I know some coaches do, but I really feel like taking a new job as the head basketball coach at a public high school is all about timing. Therefore, I accept a job with this simple rule in mind: *My coaching job is the most important head-coaching job in the nation—* believing anything less would be setting myself up for failure. Taking this approach allows me to go to work every day, roll up my sleeves, and attempt to build my program as if I were at *UCLA*.

This insures two things: first, that I am doing the absolute best job I am capable of doing at making my current program the best it can possibly become; second, that there will be opportunities for me to move on—*if and when the timing is right.*

As I have already stated, I took my first head-coaching job at Triway in 1983, thinking that I was just going to get some head-coaching experience and get back into the college game. Nineteen years later—despite what I initially thought were *the best-laid plans*—I was still coaching at Triway. Those years were some of the best of my life—which means some of the fondest memories I have had in coaching would never have happened if my greatest career goal had been to move on to a *better* job.

I have been a head coach for the better part of three decades now, and I have spent all of those years at only two schools—Wooster Triway and North Canton Hoover. This might make it seem that I wouldn't have a ton of expertise in evaluating the good and bad head-coaching jobs that open each year. Instead, I would like to suggest that taking certain important factors into consideration when job opportunities have arisen helped me to stay at Triway until the timing was right for my family and me to make the move to North Canton Hoover.

Timing is everything when making a move, and part of timing is a coach's ability to distinguish between a good job and a job that could be a dead end. Without question, there are certain head-coaching jobs that offer better opportunities at building a program than others, and there are several components of an available job that I would encourage any coach to examine before deciding whether or not to first pursue, then accept it.

Before even sending out a resume and letter of interest, there is research that I would do to make sure the available job passes the initial test. To me, there is no sense in seeking an interview if I know beforehand I don't really want the job. The test I give consists of several pretty basic questions that can be researched with relative ease:

First question: Are there athletes in the district? When I ask this question, I am not necessarily hung up on the win-loss records of each level of a program the previous year. In an ideal situation, the teams at the ninth grade and middle school levels would be having some success, but that's not the bottom line in my eyes. This question is more about the history of the district.

If there have been athletes in the district in the past, I believe that there will always be athletes, at least to the degree that success can be had on the basketball court. Of course to achieve consistent success, the athleticism that is available must be nurtured and developed into basketball talent through the structured program that my staff and I would be implementing. I know this sounds like I am over-simplifying, but *the best-laid plans* for player development insure long-term success for a program—*if* the athletes are available.

The second question I ask refers to league affiliation. Does the program fit well in its conference? In other words, can the program compete or do the other schools in the conference have far greater resources to the point that the playing field is hopelessly tilted? When I ask this question, again, I am not fixated on the record that the varsity team has had in the recent past; I am way more interested in how a particular program has historically been able to compete with the teams in its conference. If a program has been able to have success in a conference in the past, I believe that *my best-laid plans* will make that program competitive again in the not-too-distant future.

Besides the ability for my program to be competitive, there are some other questions I would want answered about the conference. Will the league present enough challenge once we become established to prepare us for tournament play? Is there a natural rival or two in the league that really generates a high degree of interest from even the most casual fan—a rivalry that creates a standing-room-only crowd, regardless of records? Is the league geographically friendly or will we be spending countless hours on a bus traveling to far-reaching schools, with no following? I wouldn't consider negative answers to any *one* of those added questions about the league to be *deal-breakers*, but I would hope to find positive answers to *most* of them.

Similarly, I would closely examine the tournament trail that my new program would need to navigate to see if there would be a *legitimate* chance for our program to make it to Columbus—where *The Final Four* is played each year in the State of Ohio. I think every coach wants the opportunity to make that tournament run at the end of the season, because it is an exhilarating experience to be a part of that run, and because it is what a coach is oftentimes judged by. There is no such thing as an easy path to a *Final Four*, but it would be nice to not be set in a district where the state's top private school resides. Again, this would not necessarily be a *deal-breaker*, but a realistic chance to make a tournament run would be nice.

If I am satisfied with the information that is gathered through this preliminary look at a program from the outside, the next step is to get the resume and letter of interest out. If an interview were to be granted, I would show up with several more questions for the committee.

I believe it is as much *my* job to interview the committee as it is for them to interview me. The information they give me in that interview allows me to draw my final conclusions on whether or not to accept the job if it is offered to me.

The first thing I would be looking to find out in the interview is this: *Does the administration have a strong desire to back a basketball coach so he can do the things he needs to do to make it become consistently successful?* To me, this *is the most important question* in deciding whether or not I would be willing to undertake the task of leading a program. Very simple reason: Without administrative support, a coach has no chance to survive, much less to be successful—a point Coach Kramer will illustrate in his section.

In my interview at Triway, I tried to gauge the committee's level of interest in me and its basketball program the same way I would measure the level of interest a friend of mine had in a particular topic of conversation—that is, were they really listening or were their minds somewhere else. We've all been in conversations where we sense the other party is losing interest. If I had sensed the people at Triway had not been *sincerely* interested in hearing my plan to rebuild their ailing basketball program, I would have never accepted the job. I knew there was going to be building to do, and I knew I would need tremendous administrative support if I were to ever enjoy the fruits of my *best-laid plans.*

I watched the level of attentiveness given to me by the administrators, and it was easy for me to see that Triway was hungry for a winning basketball program. Every member of the committee seemed to be hanging on my every word, and I sensed that they would let me run the program as I saw fit. When I left the interview at Triway, I felt the job would be a great fit for me.

Over the years, I was fortunate to work for a number of outstanding administrators who nurtured my crazy ideas and helped me develop my coaching career. I feel like I would be remiss to not list the truly great ones by name: Superintendent Jim Watson—the man who first hired me; Superintendent Tom Shoup—who hired me at Hoover; and Mike Gallina—the tremendous superintendent who took over for Tom Shoup. Principals: Lew Bevington and Tony Pallija; and Athletic Directors Sean Carmichael, Joe Eaton and Don Shimek. These are the type of men every head coach should be lucky enough to find in those key positions of leadership.

Beyond reading the attentiveness of the administration during the interview, how else can a coach get a feel for the commitment the school has to the program? Simple: ask more questions.

There are some basic questions I ask in my first interview, the answers to which would give a pretty clear picture of the type of support a coach would likely be given in a new job. Here are a few:

1. Will I have the freedom to choose my staff by putting any holdovers from the old regime into positions I see fit and by bringing assistants with me?

2. Are there athletes in the program at various levels?

3. Are season tickets sold? (This helps with regular attendance and excitement.)

4. Do we have a locker room area that can be *just* for basketball?

5. What will my teaching assignment be?

6. Will I be allowed to raise funds to be used for the basketball program—as I see fit?

7. Is the league a good fit for our basketball program?

8. Will the district give me credit for all of my years?

These are the types of questions that I would ask, and without going into a whole lot of detail about possible responses, I think it's fairly easy to see how the answers would reveal an administration's level of commitment to a basketball coach. Of course, the more of these questions that *are* answered positively by the administration, the higher the likelihood that there will be a large contingent of exceptional candidates for the job. In these cases, a coach with no head-coaching resume is at a distinct disadvantage.

Hence, the coach who is seeking his first head-coaching job needs to look for a situation where enough of the variables I have mentioned *are* positive to make him feel like his great effort and *the best-laid plans* would allow him to overcome the variables that are *not* in his favor.

When searching for a first job, rarely will everything be perfect, and it wasn't at Triway. For example, there was no locker room area specific to the basketball team when I interviewed there, and there was limited space available in the building. After doing a little searching, I found an old dusty room that nobody was using and the people at Triway allowed me to do as I pleased to make it into a place the basketball players could call a second home. None of it would have been possible without the tremendous support I received from the administration.

Another thing I like to know in the interview is whether or not the administration understands that a coach's teaching schedule needs to be conducive to performing all of his daily basketball duties. Certainly, I am not implying that a coach ought to have an *easy* schedule; however, an administration that is committed to the excellence of its athletic program understands that a coach needs to be given a schedule that will allow him to perform the vast coaching duties that come with the job on a year-round basis. The extent to which a school can meet the scheduling needs of a head coach will vary depending on staffing and size of the district, but something as simple as making sure a head coach has the final period of the day off to prepare for practice shows that the administration understands what the coach does is significant *beyond* the walls of the classroom.

One final major aspect of a school district I look at before I consider accepting a job deals with community and school funding. The question here is twofold: *Does the community show it values education by supporting school funding? If yes, is the community a place I want to live and am I comfortable sending my own kids to school in the district?*

This issue is one of the most important for me, because my family has always been so much a part of my career. Triway was a great small-town community that valued education and supported athletics, and I believe my kids were given a chance to gain a solid foundation while they began their schooling there. When I moved to North Canton, I am certain my daughters received a top-notch high school education at Hoover.

I know a coach can't always be picky, especially in his efforts to get that first job. But I can say with the utmost certainty that the two districts in which I have been the head coach have been well supported by the community—and that just makes it much easier to establish roots and lead a program.

After looking at all of the variables that go into finding a good head-coaching opportunity, I would summarize the process like this: When searching for a job as a head basketball coach at a public high school, a coach should be careful to do his research regarding the situation, but not so careful that he eliminates a potentially great opportunity. That's the basic approach I took when I sought and found my first job at Triway, and with a lot of effort and perseverance it turned out great for almost two decades—right up until the day the *timing was right* for my next challenge at North Canton Hoover.

100 (Kramer)

Coach Montgomery has made two choices in selecting head-coaching opportunities that have worked out incredibly well for him during his Hall-of-Fame career. The list of questions he shared is a great tool that every coach should use *to help* in evaluating a potential job opportunity. After eight enjoyable years as the head coach at *Fairless High*

School, I made sure to use all of those questions to help myself evaluate the opportunity I was being offered to become the head basketball coach at Canton South High School in the spring of 2008. Here's what I found.

1. *Staff selection*: I was told I could select my staff as I saw fit. I knew there were some capable assistants in the district who I would consider, and I also knew that I could bring a top assistant with me from Fairless; staff selection—*check*.

2. *Athletes*: Whereas the talent at the upper levels was not typical *South* talent, there *seemed* to be enough to be respectable while waiting on a solid eighth-grade class to develop into a group that would restore the glory of the past; athletes—*check, sort of*.

3. *Fan base*: The community *fancied itself* a basketball community, and there was a solid season-ticket base; community support—*check*.

4. *Locker room and other facilities*: At South, the facilities were solid, including a well-kept gymnasium and a locker room exclusive to basketball, complete with custom-made wooden locker stalls that looked nice and were highly functional. And there were easy ways to make relatively inexpensive improvements; facilities—*check*.

5. *Teaching assignment*: My teaching assignment would be to 'team teach' with my junior varsity coach, Eric Brickwood, essentially leaving a great deal of flexibility in my day to carry out my duties as a head coach; teaching assignment—*check*.

6. *Fund-raising*: There was a basketball account, but it had a balance of less than $100 in it when the job was offered to me. I was, however, promised the athletic department had money for summer shootouts and camps available to bridge the gap until I could raise funds specifically for my program; freedom to raise funds and use them as I saw fit—*check*.

7. *League affiliation*: The Northeastern Buckeye Conference (NBC) had always been a challenging, yet winnable league for South's good teams; league affiliation—*check*.

8. *Finances and Family*: The job was financially and family friendly. Canton South offered me all fifteen of my years on the pay scale, meaning I would be receiving a substantial raise; and my house was located less than a mile from the high school, which would reduce the amount of time I would have to spend away from my family—at least in theory; financially prudent and family friendly—*check*.

Yes, according to Coach Montgomery's list of eight questions, deciding to accept the Canton South job looked like a lay-up. So in late May of 2008, I accepted the offer to become the head basketball coach at Canton South High School—the place where *my best-laid plans* had me spending the remaining decade or so of my coaching career.

Fast Forward to March 28, 2011—thirty-four months after accepting the job...

I was in my classroom finishing up my last English class of the day when I received the following email from my athletic director at exactly 12:47 p.m.:

"Matt, you need to meet with the principal, the superintendent and myself in the conference room at 2:00 p.m. today."

It was not unusual for the athletic director and principal to want to evaluate a coach at the end of a season, so at first I didn't think too much of the email. However, as I left my classroom and walked toward my office to change clothes for my daily cardio workout on the exercise bike, I wondered what the superintendent could possibly want. She had just moved into the position the previous July, and she had never taken the time to talk to me about the basketball program; I had come to believe she was hands-off when it came to athletics.

Although her impending presence in the meeting disturbed me, I remembered that I had just talked to my building principal the previous week about my program and its progress, and he told me that he felt I had done a great job of handling a really difficult process; he told me he liked the young players we had in the program and the way they were developing, and he told me I had his full support moving forward.

In many cases, I wouldn't put too much stock in a principal's assessment of my basketball program, but this principal had won a state championship in girls' basketball during his days as a highly successful head coach, so I knew he had a very good understanding of what he was seeing and hearing. Knowing that he respected my program and the job I was doing made me feel good moving forward, and it allowed me to relax my mind and head to the bike for my workout.

After riding the bike for a good forty minutes, I walked to my office, quickly changed into a dry t-shirt, and made it to the main office at 1:58. With two minutes to spare, I decided to head into the office of my principal to see if he could quickly fill me in as to the agenda of the meeting. When I asked him what the meeting was about, he blankly responded, "What meeting?"

I told him I had received an email shortly before 1:00 p.m. stating that I was to meet with the athletic director, superintendent and him at 2:00 p.m. in the conference room. He had no idea what I was talking about—none!

As I began to get very nervous, the superintendent walked into the principal's office where I was still standing, and—without acknowledging me—she told him that he was wanted immediately in the conference room for a meeting. When she left, we looked at each other quizzically for a moment; then, without another word spoken, we both walked around the corner and toward the room where the meeting was to take place.

I was the first one to actually walk into the room and sit down, and the thirty seconds or so I had to contemplate what was going on made me feel a little bit like what an old dog must feel like when he is dragged into the vet's office—I wasn't exactly sure what was going to happen, but I was pretty sure it wasn't something I was going to enjoy. To make matters worse, none of the 'vets' in this meeting were the ones who had taken care of me in the past.

My thoughts momentarily wandered to the fact that the athletic director who had reached out to hire me had moved on, becoming the proprietor of a pub and banquet hall; the principal who had hired me had moved on to become the superintendent at another school district; and the superintendent who had been most enthusiastic about bringing me back to become the head coach had come down with an illness that caused her to step away from the rigors of the superintendent's position. Yes, within a two-year timeframe, the school district where I intended to spend the rest of my teaching and coaching career had a new athletic director, a new principal and a new superintendent, and for the first time since those transitions had become complete—sitting in that chair in the conference room—I was acutely aware of the island upon which I was standing.

Interrupting that lonely thought, the superintendent entered the room next, opening a planner as she sat down directly across from me. The principal had been approached in the hallway by someone and was in conversation about an unrelated manner just outside the door, so the superintendent began to make small talk with me about the bizarre nature of Ohio's March weather. Uneasily, I obliged and engaged her because I could see she, too, was uncomfortable, and after about a minute of enduring the palpable tension, some of the stress was lifted when the principal finally did enter the room.

After he sat down in the chair directly to my left, he looked at the super-intendent and asked, "What's up?"

As she mindlessly flipped through the planner, she responded, "Let's wait until the athletic director gets here."

No sooner than she said those words, the athletic director entered the room and took a seat—without so much as looking at me—one chair to the left of the principal. What came next did not take long, but it will be a moment of my life forever branded on my memory. The superintendent looked directly at me with a smile that seemed like her effort at compassion, and she said,

"Well... (long pause)... I don't think I have the support to recommend you to the board to continue as our basketball coach."

It was a punch in the gut that caused me to release what I can best remember being an abrupt, sarcastic laugh; then, dead silence hung over the room with the weight of a grand piano. Staring at my superintendent's face as her eyebrows had become questioningly raised, out of my peripheral vision I saw my principal's shoulders slouch forward after he had slung his face straight down to stare at his feet.

This heavy silence—which probably lasted no more than fifteen seconds—seemed like it provided me a calendar month to ponder what had gone wrong...

That's right, I was fired—so much for *the best-laid plans.* It happened on Monday, March 28, 2011 at just past 2:00 p.m., and some four months later I was finally able to get a grip and say the words—*I was fired.* It's actually quite therapeutic to be able to say *those* words, liberating even. I mean, honestly, it is every coach's worst nightmare to be fired, and many who have never experienced it live in fear of the possibility. I have now been fired and I am living to tell about it.

There, I said it again—and the thing is, I was fired after I thought this book was a finished product. I mean it was done—complete. We were going to the publisher with our text when it happened.

It's kind of ironic that it happened this way, because after reading the entire text, Coach Montgomery told me he felt like we had *definitely* covered all of the bases while keeping the book a relatively quick read. When he said this, I just sensed he was wrong—that something was missing. Then it hit me: There was nothing in the book about being fired—so I figured *I'd* step up and cover that final base.

Of course I am being sarcastic here, but some truth definitely lies within what I have said in jest. I obviously did not *martyr* myself as the head coach at Canton South High School to create a more complete book; also, it will probably become apparent to anyone who reads this book that being fired did not sit well with me.

In fact, my firing led to the toughest months I have ever experienced in my professional life. Being fired is something I never *expected* to experience—especially after winning a number of *championships* and *coach-of-the-year* awards. However, having now fully experienced *it*, I believe there are some lessons for others to learn from my mistakes and perhaps a couple of variables to consider that Coach Montgomery's list of questions in evaluating a potential job do not cover—variables that ultimately led to what I *allowed* to happen to me.

Why did I choose the word *allowed*? Simple: Before a coach can become the CEO of a basketball program, he must first take great care to be the CEO of his own career. Being a successful CEO is all about having impeccable success with making the most important decisions, and I cannot think of a more important decision a head coach makes than deciding whether or not to accept a job offer. In retrospect, had I taken the time to more carefully consider *all* of the variables, I would never have left the program that I had built and grown to love in my eight years at Fairless High School to take the Canton South job.

Knowing that I have never worked harder—or longer hours—in my career than I did at Canton South, I came to the conclusion that Coach Montgomery's list of questions must not have taken all variables into account. Upon further review, here are two questions I added that I believe completes the list:

Last Line of Defense Questions:

(Final prevention from making a poor career choice)

1. Does the school I'm considering have a history of being patient with its coaches, or do those in charge fire quickly when success is not immediate?

2. Does the district have stability amongst its administration or is there a high likelihood of impending changes in positions key to the support of a basketball coach?

If a coach were to be unfamiliar with a school district he was considering, an answer to the first question I listed above would take some research; regretfully, I must admit that my professional experience provided all the information that I needed to answer this question before I took the job at Canton South, and I was too naïve to pay attention to it. Allow me to explain:

As I have mentioned, Coach Henry Cobb was instrumental in getting me my first teaching interview at Faircrest Middle School—the feeder middle school for Canton South High School—when *he* took the head-coaching position at Canton South in June of 1993. After interviewing, I was offered the job and I spent the first seven years of my teaching career at Faircrest Middle School where I taught seventh-grade language arts while serving on Henry Cobb's staff. That seven-year stretch was the beginning of what became a '*golden decade*' of Canton South Wildcat basketball, and it did not happen by accident.

It takes a number of different ingredients for a basketball program to have a high level of consistent success over time, and some of those ingredients may vary over the course of a ten-year span; however, the following two ingredients must be constant: *good talent and good coaching.*

From 1993-2003 Canton South had really good talent, and Henry Cobb was a really good coach. In fact, from 1993 until I took my first head coaching job at Fairless High School in 2000, I witnessed Henry Cobb masterfully run the program as a member of his staff; then, from 2000 through 2003 I watched Canton South put the wraps on a decade of dominance as Henry Cobb coached the program to an unprecedented three straight *Canton Division-II District Championships*—the third one in 2003 leading to Canton South's third ever *Regional Championship* and trip to Columbus for Ohio's *Division-II Final Four.*

After a couple of so-so twelve-win seasons in 2004 and 2005—at least compared to the bar that had been set—Coach Cobb led the program back into the district title game in 2006, losing to a Triway team that would go on to play in the *state* title game. So, *actually*, for the better part of thirteen years, Canton South—along with Coach Montgomery's Triway teams—had become the gold standard for *Division-II* basketball in Northeast Ohio.

There are two reasons I have chosen *here* to highlight the decade I termed a '*golden decade*' for *Canton South Wildcat basketball*: one, to show what *led up to* Henry Cobb taking over the South program for this *golden decade*; two, to show what led to *the end* of Henry Cobb's highly

44

successful fifteen-year tenure at the school. Both scenarios go directly to answering the first *Last Line of Defense* question: *Does the school I'm considering have a history of being patient with its coaches, or do those in charge fire quickly when success is not immediate?*

Before going into the way Henry Cobb's ultra-successful tenure at South ended, I'm going to backtrack and review the three years leading up to its beginning. The coach who preceded Henry Cobb was a fantastic educator—and even better person—by the name of Jack Fuller. Coach Fuller was a Canton South alumnus who had played for *"Red" Ash*—South's legendary 500-win coach—in the 1970's. In fact, Jack was a fantastic two-sport athlete who was inducted into the *Canton South Athletic Hall of Fame* following his graduation. I came to know Jack Fuller quite well, because we taught closely together at Faircrest Middle School the seven years I assisted Henry Cobb at Canton South.

As one might expect, there was an initial obstacle between Jack and me becoming friends—the fact that he was the *fired* coach at Canton South, and I was an assistant coach for the man who replaced him. But Jack was a true professional and an inherently friendly person—plus both of us were die-hard Cleveland Indians, Cavaliers, and Browns fans. So it was just a matter of time before Jack Fuller became a friend and mentor to me in the early stages of my *teaching* career.

When he and I first started to *really* talk, I was careful to never talk *Canton South* basketball, because I knew being relieved of his head-coaching duties had been difficult for him. However, after months of talking *teaching* and *Cleveland sports*, Jack and I attended a three-day professional workshop together, and he opened up and decided he *wanted* to tell me about the way things unraveled for him as South's head coach.

Of course there is no way I could possibly remember every word of a conversation from almost twenty years ago, and I cannot go back and ask Jack to rehash it for me because he passed away in the summer of 2001, but here are the nuts and bolts of the conversation:

After spending his life living to be a Canton South Wildcat—as a young boy, as a player and as an assistant coach—Jack was awarded the opportunity to become the head basketball coach at his alma mater in 1987. He took over a program that had a good tradition, but one that had become mediocre during the 1980's. So Jack Fuller's first couple of seasons—with less than average varsity talent—his teams were mediocre, too.

Then, in 1990—only his third season as the head coach—he won the *Northeastern Buckeye Conference Title*, the *Canton Division-II District*

Title, the *Youngstown Division-II Regional Title*, and earned a trip to Canton South's second-ever *State Final Four*. Most *successful* coaches toil a lifetime and never get close; Jack Fuller got his team to Columbus for the *Final Four* in three years. *Logically*, one would have to believe his ability to lead had been well established, and his job security a given.

Well, I've already established that I went to Canton South to join *Henry Cobb's* staff in the spring of 1993, so *logic* apparently had nothing to do with job security at Canton South. Jack Fuller was fired as the head basketball coach at South in the spring of 1993—approximately three years after coaching the Wildcats to the Ohio *Division-II Final Four*. And he was fired because South had a three-year stretch following that run to the *Final Four* where they simply did not have the talent to win enough games—there was no other reason.

Jack Fuller was a man of impeccable morals and professionalism—he showed up to teach every day and put in his best effort; he showed *his best-laid plans* were plenty good enough to lead a basketball program; and the kids—students and players—loved him. He was a Canton South Wildcat to his core, but none of that was enough. After three sub-par seasons of coaching less than stellar varsity talent, the district decided Jack Fuller must have *forgotten* the things he had taught the year he took Canton South to Columbus—so he was fired.

Does the district have a history of being patient with its coaches or are those in charge quick to fire? I'd say three years is *pretty* quick, especially after a coach has established he knows what to do with talent—and especially since *Coach Fuller's best-laid plans* had worked to set up a decade of talent for his successor, Henry Cobb, when Coach Cobb arrived at Canton South in the spring of 1993.

Now, I've already said that Henry Cobb is a fantastic coach, and he is a man I consider to be instrumental in mentoring me to the success I have had in my career. My point is not to diminish any of Coach Cobb's accomplishments, because he was a *great* coach at every stop in his career. I'm simply saying that I know firsthand Jack Fuller had done a great job of developing the talent prior to Coach Cobb's arrival, because I had a chance to coach that talent with Coach Cobb.

In Henry Cobb's first season at Canton South, the sophomore class that was in place was as solid and deep a class as I've ever seen in my coaching career, and the junior class had a point guard who would be named the conference player of the year after the 1994-95 season—Coach Cobb's second season.

So the fact of the matter is this: Jack Fuller proved by taking his 1990 team to the *Final Four* that he was highly qualified to lead the *'golden decade'* of South basketball from 1993-2003, but he never got to coach the talent *his* program nurtured because he hit a three-year span where the *varsity* talent was not good enough to repeat his 1990 team's trip to the *Final Four*—at least *not quickly enough* for those in charge.

Fifteen years later, after Henry Cobb had masterfully coached Canton South to seven district title games, four *Canton Division-II District Championships*, four *NBC Championships* and earned countless *coach-of-the-year* awards, he left the job because—after one sub-par, nine-win season in 2007-08—*he* was catching *heat!* Here was a guy who had given half a career to the unprecedented success of a school, and Canton South was making things tough on *him* when they should have been pushing to have his name painted on the court in the gymnasium.

Does the district have a history of being patient with its coaches or are those in charge quick to fire? Well, Henry Cobb did *not* get fired, but he did not leave because he wanted to retire from coaching, either. And because I am not Henry Cobb, I'll leave it at that.

The point is this: If I had been looking attentively, with eyes wide open—not the starry eyes of a coach flattered by being courted to take on a new job with a nice raise—I would have seen that Canton South had a long history of being intolerant with rebuilding plans. Hence, I would have never considered even interviewing for the position when Henry Cobb resigned, because I was *definitely* walking into a rebuilding plan when I accepted the job at Canton South in 2008—a case I attempted to plead when I broke the silence back in that meeting with *the firing squad* on March 28, 2011...

Still in shock but feeling a need to say something, I looked at the superintendent and fervently explained:

"Three years ago I sat in this same room and I told Teresa Purses, Rocky Bourquin and Tom Bratten—the superintendent, athletic director and principal who hired me—that the basketball program was in bad shape." *I gasped for a breath and kept at it.* *"I reminded them my program at Fairless had become the best Division-II program in the county, and they knew it, and that's why they hired me."* *Still getting no response, I finished,* *"And I told them that I would leave my very comfortable situation at Fairless to come home here to Canton South if they understood that it was going to take time to get it going again, and they acknowledged that there was very little talent,*

and they gave me their promise that they trusted me to do what I did at Fairless, and they hired me to rebuild this basketball program, and they knew full well that meant taking a step or two back for a few years!"

After that run-on, I felt that I had made my point and that, at the very least, I had set grounds for discussion. However, after a short pause to see if I had finished to what amounted as being my closing argument, the superintendent ended with the verdict:

"Matt, I don't doubt what you're saying, but none of us were in the room that day."

And that was the end of the discussion—and my thirty-four month tenure as the head coach at Canton South High School…

Canton South *definitely* had a history of being extremely impatient with its head basketball coaches over the years—a point made in the firing of Jack Fuller in 1993, three years after a trip to the *Final Four*; a point reinforced in Henry Cobb's sudden resignation after *one* mediocre season at the end of a *stellar* fifteen-year tenure; and a point hammered home by *my* firing less than three years into an elaborate rebuilding project.

Now, I don't necessarily believe that a coach should refuse a potential job *solely* because a school has a history of being impatient with coaches; however, I do believe such a history requires a coach to go back to Coach Montgomery's second question and revise it like this:

Are there enough athletes to win a reasonable number of games at the varsity level—right now?

I believe a *clear* 'no' response coupled with the knowledge that a school has a history of being *very* impatient with basketball coaches constitutes *a good reason* for a coach to refuse a job. Had I thought it all the way through, I would have seen it coming—and I never would have left Fairless.

Knowing there wasn't enough talent to satisfy the immediate needs of a historically impatient basketball school should have been enough to keep me from leaving the stability of the solid program I had built over eight years at Fairless; it should have been enough to keep me from walking into the disaster that the Canton South job was when I took it. And that's what I meant earlier in this section when I said I *allowed* my firing to happen.

This brings me to the second of my two *Last Line of Defense* questions: *Does the district have stability amongst its administration or is there a high likelihood of impending changes in positions key to the support of a basketball coach?*

The following fact kept me from becoming bitter after being fired. Not one person in the room the day I was fired had anything to do with hiring me—not one. And the only one in the room that had taken the time to get to know me and understand where the program was, and where it was headed, was the principal—a man by the name of Todd Osborn. Not coincidentally, he was the only one of the three in the room who had any idea what he was seeing and hearing when it came to my basketball program because—as I mentioned—he was a former accomplished head girls' basketball coach. Todd Osborn had nothing to do with my firing, evidence being that he found out about the meeting in which I was to be fired two minutes before it took place.

So it really came down to the athletic director and the superintendent, whose names I will keep anonymous because the purpose of sharing this is not to designate blame. With what was certain to have been a good bit of influence from one particular board member who took a special disliking to me, the new athletic director and the new superintendent decided they were going to hire *their* guy to be the basketball coach; the fact that neither the athletic director nor the superintendent had *ever* had a conversation with me about the state of the program leads me to *suspect* that they had made their decision before the season ever started. Of course that *is* simply speculation on my part—based on the fact that we had shown dramatic improvement in my third and final season.

Anyone who was paying attention could see the improvement from 2009-10 to 2010-11. We made a six-win improvement on our record from the previous season, and again, we were very young, lettering four sophomores and a freshman—with our sophomore point guard, Armand Fontes, being our first *All-NBC* selection in two years. And to make matters more encouraging, I looked forward to welcoming a class to the high school that had won the league championship as eighth graders—a group that was comprised of one fantastic scoring guard, one fantastic wing player, and a variety of really solid complementary players.

In my mind, *the best-laid plans* were right on course: We would jump to the ten to thirteen-win mark in 2011-12, then we'd get over the hump and start really rolling in 2012-13—and beyond. It had worked that way at Fairless in my first head-coaching job, and I was confident in my mind that I was seeing it working again at Canton South—it was exactly what I was hired to do.

Unfortunately, my mind didn't get a vote; in fact, the only votes that counted were those belonging to the *new* superintendent and the *new* athletic director. Had there not been a complete overhaul in those two key positions, I am confident I would have had the opportunity to see my plan through at Canton South.

And here's the tough part about asking the second *Last Line of Defense* question: Honestly, the people who hired me thought they would be at Canton South for the better part of the next ten years—at least. The athletic director when I was hired was a *Canton South lifer*, a man many considered to be *the* face of Canton South High School—*The Godfather of Canton Township*; likewise, the superintendent was a highly respected professional in the middle of a successful tenure leading the school district. Both people were *where* they wanted to be, and they both reached out to me to lead the basketball program; nobody could have foreseen the circumstances that arose that took the two of them away from Canton South to different places in their careers. When I accepted the job, it appeared they were going to be at Canton South forever. Life *happened*, and it didn't work that way.

Looking at my experience with being fired, there are some conclusions that can be drawn. First, as Coach Montgomery stressed in his *500-section*, administrative support is *the number one thing* a coach must have to be successful. There is no getting around it, and it doesn't matter how good the coach *is* or what he has done in the past. When those that hire and fire decide it's time for a change, a change *will be* made. There doesn't need to be a reason; it doesn't matter where the coach is in his building plan; and it doesn't matter that there is a *basketball family* that has been built—with *real* relationships from the top down. It doesn't matter that the firing will likely slow down the developmental process of *every* player in the program. None of it matters! When the administration has made up its mind, things are likely to end abruptly.

In my case, like I mentioned, I was *never* bitter—not for one second. That sounds made-up, I know—but it's true. If I had been fired by the regime that had reached out to offer me the job, you can bet I would have been bitter. My firing was a business decision made by people who did not know anything about me except the complaints I am sure they were hearing that are common from disgruntled fans and parents during a tough season. And frankly, the people that fired me did not know enough about high school basketball at the time of my firing for their opinions to be offensive to me.

Like I said earlier, I blame *me* for allowing myself to be fired, and the rest I attribute to bad luck. Would I have done *some* things differently in my three years at Canton South? Absolutely! Every coach who is any good knows there are always things that could have been done differently, even in years where success is plentiful. Would I have changed what was at the *core* of *my best-laid plans*? Absolutely not! My approach was tested and triumphant at Fairless High School where I spent the first eight years of my head-coaching career, and it was on the verge of paying off at Canton South. The most important thing once the firing happened was to deal with *it* in a dignified and classy manner—a challenge made even more difficult by the immediate circumstances I found myself in.

The night I was fired I was in the awkward position of being the coach of the East Stark County All-star Team in the annual Stark County East-West game. Wanting to be able to do right by the players on the team, I thought about waiting until I came home from coaching the All-star game to tell my wife, Chris, about the firing, because—in a way—I felt like the firing wouldn't be official until I told *her*. But she sensed something odd in me within the first half-hour of being home from work and eventually asked me why I was acting strangely. I couldn't lie to her.

When I told her I had been fired, she sobbed inconsolably for about two minutes, then—with tears streaming down her face—she looked up at me and asked, "Why don't you look upset?"

I don't know if it was because I realized I had done all I could do for thirty-four months in what was a very difficult rebuilding job, or if maybe it just hadn't sunk in yet. Whatever the case may have been, I told her that I would *absolutely* bounce back and end up in a better situation for *us*. Because she is a great coach's wife, my best friend and the only person who knows how long and hard I work to devote myself to my career, she believed in my response—even if I wasn't totally sure I believed in it.

The next morning I called my dad and told him. That was hard for me, because part of what makes coaching such a satisfying career for me is the pride my dad takes in watching me do the job *he* had such a passion for doing. After his initial shock, he said something that I think every coach might want to consider before accepting a job. My dad said,

"Matt, *tradition* without players gets a coach fired."

51

I thought his quote was brilliant. At Fairless I was allowed the time to tear the program apart when it was in bad shape to rebuild it for long-term success. After two tough seasons at the varsity level, the Fairless program grew into the top achieving *Division-II* program in Stark County. At Canton South I was doing the same thing, because that's what I had been hired to do. *Tradition* simply didn't want to wait for the process to be completed at Canton South.

Once fired, the big question that I found to be nearly impossible not to ask was this: Will the program that fired me be better in the coming years? Trust me, I tried and tried to completely avoid thinking about this question—kind of like a divorced man tries to avoid wondering if his ex-wife will be happier with her new husband. But I couldn't help it—so I explored the question in hope that doing so would allow me to completely detach from wondering about it and move on.

Here's the way I answered the question in my mind without being self-serving: I believe wholeheartedly in the plan I was leading and the work I put in at Canton South. I knew that the program was developing bit by bit—at a solid pace. I know my staff and I worked our *asses* off for thirty-four months at creating a feeder system all the way down to kindergarten, and we worked just as relentlessly at the development of the young players at the high school level—a collection of future three and four-year lettermen who would head into their sophomore and junior seasons with a ton of varsity experience in 2011-12. Hence, I believe my three years at Canton South gives the next coach a reasonably good place to pick things up and implement his own plan for achieving success. That's as much *predicting* as I believe I have the right to do, and where it goes from there is anyone's guess.

Of course, any coach who has experienced being fired knows the harsh truth: There is a long list of coaches who have toiled to rebuild only to be fired just short of enjoying the fruits of *their best-laid plans*. In many cases, another coach comes in, does a good job of picking it up, and leads the program to success. Other times, one firing leads to another firing and a school or organization wanders blindly through the wilderness of consistent losing created by the instability that is the product of impatience. Regardless of which way it goes from here at Canton South, I will not try to explain away any blame people want to place on me; I will claim no victories in the work I did at Canton South; and I will harbor no bitterness toward anyone.

What has allowed me to handle the experience of being fired in a classy and dignified manner? Two things: first, writing about *it* has allowed me to sort through my feelings and put things into proper perspective; second, I leaned on the best coach's wife in the world and loving family, a father who has gone through the same thing, and the two great friends I have in coaching, Randy Montgomery and Tim Vick.

Admittedly, the process of healing from my firing has been difficult, but I believe it has made me a better *CEO* of my own career, and I believe it will make me an even better *CEO* for the next program I have the opportunity to run.

As for the coaches out there who have gone through their own firing, if reading about my experience did not lead you to a deeper understanding of why it happened to you, then I hope it at least was a way for you to commiserate with a colleague who definitely understands what you went through. Sometimes that can be the most comforting thing.

For the coaches out there who have never been fired, some of whom may even be searching for that first head-coaching opportunity, I think it's important for you to remember this: Before a coach becomes the *CEO* of his program, he is first the *CEO* of his own career. A bad choice selecting a job often makes *doing that job* an impossible feat. I hope that Coach Montgomery and I have offered some things in this section that will help all coaches make prudent decisions in selecting a job that is the right fit.

Review of Questions to Ask in Evaluating a Job:

Initial 8 Questions:

1. Will I have the freedom to choose my staff by putting any holdovers from the old regime into positions I see fit and by bringing an assistant with me?

2. Are there athletes in the program at various levels?

3. Are season tickets sold? If not, can we start selling them?

4. Do we have a locker room area that can be just for basketball?

5. What will my teaching assignment be?

6. Will I be allowed to raise funds to be used for the basketball program as I see fit?

7. Is the league a good fit for the basketball program?

8. Will the district compensate me fairly according to my experience?

If questions 1-8 check out, Last Line of Defense Questions:

9. Does the school district have a history of being impatient with its coaches, firing when success is not immediate? *(If yes, revise question #2: Are there enough athletes to win right now?)*

10. Are the administrators who hired me likely to stay long enough for me to get the program stabilized?

5

First Days on the Job:

Locker rooms & Wizards;
Cookouts & Logos

---

500 (Montgomery)

SINCE MY FIRST head-coaching tenure at Triway lasted nineteen years, I went into my second job at North Canton Hoover with the idea that I was in it for the long haul. How did that affect the way I spent my first days on the job? I focused on the skill development and recruitment of the next generation of *my* basketball players—and I went to work on building a *tradition*.

I started by asking myself: *What is basketball's most important fundamental skill?* Many coaches would argue the answer is *shooting*; I say it's *ball handling*. I'm not minimizing the importance of being able to put the ball in the basket, but I have found that it does a team very little good to have shooters if the players are unable to maneuver the ball adeptly into places on the floor where good shots can be found. Therefore, the first part of *the best-laid plans* was to introduce a *fun* program that would build ball-handling skills in every prospective player—from kindergarten through sixth grade.

Where did I find such a program? I stumbled across the *Holy Grail* of ball handling programs while attending a game back in 1985 at the Canton Memorial Field House between *Canton McKinley* and *Blackhawk High School* from Pennsylvania.

That night, Blackhawk High School just happened to have brought its 'Little Dribblers' on the road trip to Canton with its varsity team so the little guys could perform at halftime of the varsity game. The head coach at Blackhawk was *John Miller*, and one of the little dribblers was none other than *Sean Miller*—yes the Sean Miller who starred at the University of Pittsburgh in the late 1980's and early 1990's; the one who coached Xavier University to a couple of *NCAA "Sweet-16"* appearances; and the one who currently holds the *prestigious* job as head coach at the University of Arizona.

When halftime came, my wife Becky and I were in awe at what these *little* kids from Blackhawk were doing with the basketball, so I decided—on the spot—that *I* was going to implement a similar program. I *immediately* took the idea back to Triway—where I had already been the head coach for two years—and it became a *major* hit.

The Wizards program built ball-handling skills in generations of Triway players—that much I expected. What I did *not* expect was that the performances by The Wizards—which started out as a curiosity for those watching at halftime of *our* games—became entertainment *sought after* by some pretty *big-time* organizations.

During the seventeen years the program ran at Triway, *The Wizards* performed at *Notre Dame* games, *Cleveland Cavaliers* games, *Penn State* games, *The Macy's Parade*, and a variety of smaller venues. How many second graders get a chance to do those things? Yes, it was *fun* to be a *Triway Wizard*.

Like it was at *rural* Triway, success at *suburban* Hoover will *always* be about skill, so I spent my first days on the job there working to launch the little-dribblers concept for my new program. First, I knew that I was going to need a special person who had to love teaching youth the fundamentals of handling the basketball—and create a fun environment in which to do it.

At Triway, I was fortunate that a *basketball man* named Gene Gottfried stepped forward to get *The Wizards* off to a great start. Gene then passed the torch to a man named Jack Henley and, over the years, *Jack* was the one that took it to another level.

Without those two men, much of what was accomplished at Triway would not have been a possibility. Hence, step one to launching *The Hoopsters*—the name given to the Hoover version of *The Wizards*—was finding the same type of enthusiastic and dedicated leadership that had been in place at Triway. When I found him—a man named John Lucas—he was the first person I added to my staff at Hoover. John's energetic and innovative approach set *The Hoopsters* program in full swing at Hoover, where—just like at Triway—it has *continued* to be key to the success of my program.

If the little-dribbler program is step *1-A* on the to-do list once I start a new job, then putting my personal stamp on the locker room is step *1-B*. If the locker room is a dirty old smelly room—a place where players want to spend as little time as possible—the tone has been set for that to be the approach by the players toward the *entire* basketball experience.

I want the locker room to be a very special place—a place where kids consider it a *privilege* to spend time. When I interviewed at both Triway back in the 1980's and Hoover in 2002, I *insisted* that we had our *own* area. I told the interviewing committee that the space could be any-where and any size, but I wanted it to be *ours* so I could begin to build *tradition*.

When I accepted the job at Triway, the administration honored my locker room wish and gave me a dusty old hot room that nobody had used since the advent of the zone defense—and the work started. One of my player's fathers—a man who said that he wasn't good at bake sales but could swing a hammer—built and paneled the whole room. With the completion of *that* locker room, the Triway tradition—a tradition that is still *highly* regarded around the State of Ohio—was born.

I was so proud of that locker room the day it was finished, but I took even more pride in it as it developed over my stay at Triway. We took a dust closet and created what I felt was *the* nicest high school locker room in Ohio. And it had all the amenities: a stereo, a big screen for film review, professionally displayed motivational quotes in each locker, and our *Big Game Board* that listed all the big wins we enjoyed over the years—and there was more.

Steve Burgess—who was an assistant with Dan Peters and me on Bob Huggins' staff at *Walsh College* in 1981—is an accomplished artist who has helped many programs by painting and adding personality to their locker rooms. One very unique thing Steve and I created at Hoover is a large wooden 'wishing well' that has magnetic numbers attached that keeps a tally of our home court record—a new way we invented to build tradition. Changing the number in the "W" column after every game has now become a time-honored ritual at Hoover— after eight seasons it reads 72-4. Steve made *The Well* and painted the following phrase on it: *Drink the water, but remember who dug the well!* Tradition starts with *simple* ideas like this.

At Hoover, we have other items that serve as decoration and moti-vation in our locker room—things like framed letters from former players and famous coaches, including the legendary John Wooden and Ohio State football coach Jim Tressel. I also brought *The Big Game Board* idea to Hoover and—although it isn't as extensive as the one I left at Triway—it is beginning to display a significant pride in tradition.

I also use the locker room to give the seniors special attention. One way is by creating *Senior Row*—a column of lockers where only seniors reside—and *only* seniors have their names above their lockers. When a player's senior season is complete, his nameplate goes above his locker along with the team's record his senior year. *Senior Row* serves as a living history lesson of the program—not to mention as peer pressure for *every* senior that ever plays at Hoover.

Another special touch we display to honor the seniors in the locker room are 18" by 24" framed, color action pictures of *every* senior that has *ever* played in *my* time at Hoover. I want to make sure that the Hoover tradition connects the past to the present and the future—and a big part of that happens in our locker room.

It is my philosophy that if the locker room is made to be a special place, the players will begin to take ownership and pride in the program. I have seen this philosophy work at both Triway and Hoover—that's why I spent my first days on both jobs working to develop a locker room that would serve our players as a second home while displaying an evolving tradition.

Locker rooms and youth dribbling programs might not be the first things that coaches usually think about when hired into a new head-coaching position. But when I accept a job, those are two of the first things that get my attention—the youth dribblers so there will always be players to keep the tradition going, and the locker room so there will always be a place to display the tradition as it unfolds.

100 (Kramer)

I encourage any head coach starting a new job to consider Coach Montgomery's suggestions; the things he does in his first days on the job have led to incredible success. However, no two coaches—or situations—will be exactly the same, so I will add the ideas that worked for me given the variables that existed when I was hired into the two head-coaching positions I have held.

When the phone rang on August 2nd, 2000, and Fairless High School athletic director Renee Fogle spoke the words that I had worked my entire adult life to hear—*Matt, we'd like you to be our next head basketball coach*—I accepted while sitting by a swimming pool in Myrtle Beach, South Carolina. What does a new head coach do the first few days on the job when he's 650-some miles away from home? Simple: I tried to enjoy the last few days of vacation while obsessing over *where* I would start once I returned home. It was an exciting time, yet very unsettling, because I had never assumed leadership of a program before.

Furthermore, by the time I had returned home from the vacation, it was the second week of August—a period of non-contact for basketball coaches in the State of Ohio—so I wouldn't be able to do much more than introduce myself to my players, most of whom had started practice for a fall sport. I had prepared a lifetime to become a head coach; I was excited and ready; yet I had no players to coach. So the first lesson I would pass on to any head coach in his first days on the job is: be ready to *adapt your best-laid plans* to find a productive starting point.

Team-building activities, open gyms, skill sessions, and shootouts were off the table, so—after signing my contract and shaking hands with a number of people who would become important in my life—I filled a bag with *my* starting point: he previous season's scorebook, game films and opponents' rosters.

Looking over the Fairless roster from the previous season, I realized I *couldn't* watch *my* players on film—another disadvantage—because every point, rebound and assist from the previous season's 18-win Fairless team had graduated. But I *could* learn everything those films, scorebooks and rosters had to teach me *about my opponents*.

I started with our league opponents—the Principals Athletic Conference, or PAC-7. Finally, in a haystack of disadvantages, I found the needle I had been seeking: the league was unfamiliar with *me* and, while I could study my opponents, there were no films for my new rivals to study me. So I went to work building preliminary—yet thorough—scouting reports on every league opponent, and those reports would serve a number of purposes.

First, knowing I would have only three weeks to prepare once practice started in early November—after no summer—I knew there would be no time to teach my players to be masters of everything in a new system before our first game. So the scouting reports showed me what we absolutely *needed* to be adept at to have a chance to compete out of the gate—invaluable information in helping me shape my early practice schedules.

Next, I used the information to type scouting guides for my assistant coaches to use during the season. Since coaches are creatures of habit, my scouting guides provided my assistants with an idea of what they were *likely* to see when scouting an opponent. The job of the scout would be to take the report *I* had supplied him and check off the things on the report he saw the opponent using, plus add anything to the report the opponent had added to its approach. This method of scouting—one I have continued to use—makes creating an accurate report a more reasonable task for assistant coaches.

Finally, the scouting reports went into files that expanded over the years and provided ready-made study guides for my players, my staff and me to constantly update our familiarity with our opponents. These files paid off over the years, and they paid off in that first season.

Heading into my first season at Fairless—because I was a first-year head coach with a roster void of experience—the local newspapers predicted we would finish dead last in our conference. Instead, we finished in second place, losing in what amounted to the conference championship game to Sandy Valley High School—a game played in front of a standing-room-only crowd in *their* old *Hoosiers-style* gym—in triple overtime. Watching the Sandy Valley fans storm the floor after the final buzzer was an excruciating way to fall short, but the way it ended was *also* very gratifying.

The players on my first team came from nowhere to create their own legacy. As the season wore on, overtimes, buzzer beaters and upsets became *the norm*, and every game was a *big game* played in front of a packed house. The season captured the attention of the Fairless community and it set a tone that my teams would compete and strive for excellence regardless of who had graduated from the previous season. If I had written the script for my first season as a head coach, the *only* thing I would have changed would have been the outcome of the triple-overtime championship game.

Studying films wasn't what I would have chosen to do during the first days of my first head-coaching job—ideally, I would spend my first days as a new hire meeting my players and scheduling activities that would help us begin to *connect* and form the bonds and relationships that are so instrumental in any successful organization. But the things I *did* do in my first days on the job—my best option given the variables with which I was presented—*definitely* helped put my first team in a position to maximize its potential, and that team set a tone upon which future success would be built at Fairless.

After eight terrific years at Fairless, I accepted the job as head basketball coach at Canton South High School—this time in late May. Accepting the South position *in May* afforded me more starting options, but it still wasn't perfect. Again, I faced disadvantages that forced me to find a starting point that would launch my new program.

What were the disadvantages? The biggest was that the summer schedule had already been set—most head coaches complete their summer calendars and send out deposits and fees before the beginning of May—so I was stuck with a calendar that I knew wouldn't be conducive to the growth of my new program. But it was my job to make it work, so I decided I was going to do four things with my new program at Canton South my first days on the job in the summer of 2008:

1.   Scout the previous season's game films—just as I had done at Fairless.

2.   Begin fostering a *basketball-family* environment by creating relationship-building activities around the schedule that had been set.

3.   Develop a mindset in the players that we were going to play fast—at a *Phoenix Suns* pace.

4.   Introduce *our brand* by creating a basketball-specific logo.

The first thing on the list has already been explained in detail. Scouting the game films in my first days on the job at Fairless created a clear picture of our opponents for that first season, and it started folders on our opponents that were useful throughout my eight-year tenure there. I would make it a part of my first days on any new coaching job.

The second idea on my list is tricky, because there is no blueprint for building solid relationships with high school basketball players. But I had experienced success with it at Fairless—many people considered me a player's coach—so I immediately decided to start making an effort to nurture the program into a *basketball family* at Canton South.

The day after I accepted the position, Rocky Bourquin, the athletic director, introduced me to the returning players and I was ready with a message that would begin to establish the type of relationships with them that I felt would be vital to my coaching style:

Boys—I addressed them—*I love the game of basketball; it has been a huge part of my life. However, the relationships I build with my players are far more important to me than anything that happens on the basketball court. When that is no longer true*—I stressed—*I will no longer coach.*

I *said* that to the players because I *meant* it. For me, it has to be that way. Every coach spends far more time with players off the court than they do on the court, so it makes sense to make sure the players know *they* are the most important thing to me—*not* winning basketball games.

After verbalizing that message to the players, I went to work *showing* them I meant it. As I stated, most of what was on the summer calendar had already been set and paid for, and I knew breaking commitments would have strained my relationship with the surrounding basketball communities. I knew my job was to find ways to turn positives into negatives.

The first weekend of the summer contact period we honored a commitment to play in a local shootout I knew would be unproductive for us, because I was bringing a completely different style of play to the program, and my players were only going to have one or two sessions to learn our new style before playing some pretty stiff competition. So I decided to have a cookout and campfire at my house for the players *after* the shootout to make sure something positive came out of the day.

The cookout is a simple idea—one I used many times with my players at Fairless over the years—and one I certainly don't believe I invented. However, don't underestimate the power of a team function like this. I grilled burgers and hotdogs, some of the kids' parents sent desserts, and we had pop and Gatorade. Since I am fortunate enough to live on a sizable piece of land, I also made a campfire to sit around and just socialize with the guys. Like I said, this concept is simple, it's fun, and it's a great way to get to know the players in a setting outside of basketball.

I never set a time limit on the cookout. I want the players to know they can stay at my house as long as they are enjoying themselves. As I get older, I keep expecting the year has finally come when the players would rather not spend too much time with me off the court, because there are more enjoyable things for young people to do than hang out with a *forty-something*-year-old coach. But every year I am pleasantly surprised when *I* am the guy that has to eventually say the evening is over. My first summer at South, a week after I had accepted the job, we started the cookout at 4:00 p.m., and at 11:00 p.m. I was still sitting around the fire talking about *life* with my new *basketball family.*

My next move was to try to find a date where I could add an overnight trip onto our existing schedule. Finding a shootout or team camp that still had an opening *and* fit our calendar was not easy, but we got lucky when I found that *Jamie Dixon's Team Camp* at *The University of Pittsburgh* had an opening because a team had cancelled.

The team camp at Pitt lasted three days and two nights, and it served as a place where we could continue the momentum we had started at the cookout in becoming a *basketball family*. At the camp, we played plenty of basketball but, more importantly, we ate meals together, we *lived* in the dorms together, and we hung out together. We even added a special night out together—a trip to *PNC Park* in downtown Pittsburgh to take in a *Pittsburgh Pirates* game. The three days at the University of Pittsburgh did exactly what I had hoped it would do— we returned to Canton South a *closer* group.

These activities are never about the hamburger or the baseball game; in fact, they are all about spending quality time with the young men I coach so that we have some common *enjoyable* experiences outside of basketball that serve as the foundation for the relationships we will have on the floor—relationships that may otherwise become very hard for a player to understand.

My players understand that I care about them first. That's where it starts for me. Why? Because I believe that a player who knows I care about him is more likely to accept my discipline and constructive criticism, and still be willing to give his all when I ask him for all he has to give.

Building solid relationships with the players also serves another long-term purpose—it keeps negativity out of the locker room. No matter whom the coach is or how many games he wins, sooner or later he will be confronted with people who are negative toward him and the program. The key is keeping infectious negativity out of the locker room.

Consequently, the opinions about me that matter the most are the ones held by my players. If the players hold me in high esteem, it should insulate the program and me from any negativity that exists on the outside, allowing the *basketball family* to focus on important tasks in the gym.

The third idea on *my* list of things to do my first days on the job at Canton South was to instill in the players that we were going to play at a faster pace than they ever imagined they could play. Rather than spending my time cramming their heads with *X's & O's* they were unlikely to retain with any depth, I decided to use my ten instructional days allowed by the *Ohio High School Athletic Association*—our governing athletic body—to instill the concepts and attitudes required to master our fast-paced philosophy.

The toughest part of teaching the running game is developing the mindset in the players that I—the head coach—*really* want them to play *that* fast. Also, they must trust that they are going to be permitted to make some aggressive turnovers while pushing the tempo—a concept foreign to many players, because some coaches do not have it in their DNA to accept a turnover.

At Fairless, we became known for our highly effective running game and, the fact is, an occasional aggressive turnover was part of it. It's a matter of *risk-reward*, and I wanted my players to spend our time together in that first summer at Canton South exploring *their* options in the running game while *I* taught them the difference between good and bad risks.

To stress that they had the freedom to run and make aggressive mistakes, I told them I didn't care how many turnovers we made or how many summer games we won. I told them that the only thing I cared about in our summer games was that they played *hard* and they played *fast*, because I knew I would have plenty of time to build on those two things once practice started in November.

The final thing I wanted to do when I accepted the job at Canton South was introduce our new *brand* by creating a logo specific to the basketball program. I stumbled across the logo idea when I rebuilt my program during the middle years of my tenure at Fairless. It was a powerful way to market the program in my later years *there*, so I wanted to make it a way of launching my program at Canton South.

Some coaches might wonder what good this does. I believe creating a new logo served a number of purposes. First off, it allowed me to *immediately* put my personal stamp on the program—something that I think *every* new head coach wants to accomplish.

Next, it allowed me to create new gear for the players and community. The logos I created at Fairless and South—with the help of one of my former players, Jamie Salsburg, and his company Limelight Apparel—can be seen on t-shirts, sweatshirts, shorts, baseball caps, jackets, and anything else that can be embroidered or screen-printed. The players came to wear the logos proudly, and our team shop became a way of raising funds while getting the logo out into the community.

Ultimately, the basketball logo we created *at Fairless* was the symbol people associated with the *special* program we had built. It was a clear, yet subtle logo—it did not vary from the school colors and it did not attempt to separate the program from the school. But when people saw it, they thought *"Fairless Basketball"*—just like people think *"Yankees Baseball"* when they see the world-famous 'NY' logo or *"Cowboys Football"* when they see the Dallas star.

Yes, the number of people who recognize professional sports logos is far greater than the number that recognized the two logos I created, but the concept is the same: the logo we created was a constant advertisement of our basketball program, and it was all over the community. Doesn't every coach want his community thinking about his basketball program all year round?

I believe all of the things I mentioned doing in my first days on the job were positives for the two programs I have led, and my hope is that you will find some of them useful when you begin leading your program. But here's the biggest thing I would like all of you to take from *my* section: A coach *must* be willing to read *the* situation and *adapt*. The things I did in my first days on the two head-coaching jobs I held were directly related to the variables that existed when I took leadership, and that is the biggest reason they were productive.

Review Suggestions for *Your* First Days on the Job:

1. Remodel your locker room into a special place for the players.

2. Create a Little-dribblers skills program that performs at half-time of all home games and other venues.

3. Scout game film from the previous year to develop files on each opponent.

4. Create team-building activities to weave into the fabric of the basketball schedule for the purpose of beginning to nurture a basketball family.

5. Choose the one component of your system you deem most important—mine was the running game—and teach the players to begin mastering its concepts.

6. Create a basketball-specific logo to market your new program.

6

Choosing a Staff:

Loyalty from the true inner-circle

500 (Montgomery)

LOYALTY AND A willingness to work and learn is the recipe for being hired on my staff. An assistant coach needs to be totally on board, and if he's not, I sense it and I find new ones, *immediately*. A bad assistant coach can cause numerous problems, and a really bad one can even cost a head coach his job.

Since loyalty is a quality that shows itself over a period of time, I believe former players make ideal assistants, because they believe in my system and their loyalty runs very deep. Today, you see the hiring of former players in college coaching as well—look no further than *Duke*, one of the nation's top programs every year, to see an example of a bench full of assistants who are former players. The longer I coached at Triway, the more laden with former players my staff became and it was the best way, in my opinion, to build a staff.

One great example is one of my former assistants at Triway by the name of Sean Carmichael. Sean actually played on my first team at Triway and from there became an assistant coach staying with me on the bench through my long tenure there. Sean eventually became the head baseball coach and athletic director at Triway, so he wasn't a guy who came in and coached with me as a means to look for someplace bigger—his goal was to work as hard as he could to help Triway. When it came to loyalty to our program, to Triway and to *me*, it didn't get any better than Sean Carmichael.

Sean is just one great example that personifies the good fortune I have had with loyal assistants throughout my career—not all of them former players. Doran Braun was a great man and a good assistant. Ty Moorehead did a tremendous job for me at Triway as a middle school coach. I could name a ton of names, and several have gone on to their own head-coaching careers.

One of my long-time assistants, Keith Snoddy, actually helped persuade me to apply at Triway over two decades ago, then served as an assistant to me for many years there. When I left to take the job at Hoover, Keith took over as the head coach, and I watched proudly as he continued the success and tradition we had built while putting his own stamp on the program. A similar pride takes place when a former player of mine gets his shot.

Chad Pado—a player for me at Triway—continued to stay close with me after he graduated in 1994, and I was honored to be in his wedding in 2003. Two years after his wedding, he received his first chance to become a head coach when he took the job at Westlake High School. A coach who has experienced solid success in his early years, Chad Pado is one of the bright young minds in coaching today.

Another former player of mine, BJ Sanderson, coached freshmen ball for Keith Snoddy at Triway, then took over the girl's program there. BJ has also experienced solid success in his early years as a head coach, and he's not the only former player of mine who has tried things on the lady's side.

Brian Kiper—a 1991 Triway graduate—currently heads the prestigious program at Myrtle Beach High School in South Carolina where he has won a state championship.

I am grateful to the many assistants I have had over the years— almost all of whom have served me with great loyalty. They work extremely hard for me, and I do all I can in return to help them achieve their career goals. So it is always rewarding when I have the opportunity to watch their careers flourish.

Of course it is most gratifying to have my daughter, Annie, following in my footsteps as her career as a teacher and assistant basketball coach in the Hoover girl's program has begun to take off. I have experienced many thrills in coaching, but one of the greatest was having the opportunity to sit with Annie on her junior varsity bench during her first year. Family and basketball have always been so closely linked in my life, so that was awesome beyond explanation.

At Hoover, I feel like it took longer to build my staff, maybe because the recent basketball tradition had not been rich prior to my accepting the job there—or maybe it was because I just don't remember how long it took to get my staff *just* right at Triway. I do know this: Many coaches are shocked when they join my staff at how much time and work goes into being a good assistant. Therefore, the second key quality I look for in an assistant—not far behind loyalty in importance—is work ethic.

My assistants must be people who are tireless in their willingness to work and indispensable when it comes to their time.

Now that I have been at Hoover for the better part of a decade, I feel like I have an excellent staff in place—a staff consisting of dedicated, qualified, and loyal assistants to whom I have entrusted with a number of important duties. Furthermore, it is a diverse staff.

My varsity assistant, Troy Clark, is a good young assistant who carries out a number of duties on and off the court. Troy is in charge of our weight-training program, and on the floor has a big say in our defensive approach. Of course—as the head coach—I put a final stamp on everything, but Troy and I often collaborate, and the defense is *primarily* his concentration during practices and games.

Besides his on-the-court duties, I have given Troy the *complete* responsibility of organizing the match-ups for the mid-season showcase event we host at Hoover called *The Mercy Medical Classic*. Troy has done an excellent job with these match-ups and his work is a big reason that *The Classic* has become one of Ohio's top in-season showcase events. I delegate many important assignments to my top assistant, and Troy Clark handles them all with aplomb.

Another valuable member of my current staff is a man by the name of Jim York. Jim is currently my junior varsity coach and a good one. He does an outstanding job of developing our junior varsity players, and he relates well to kids of all ages—a skill he puts on display when he directs our summer youth skills camp. Jim is also proof you do not need to have a doctorate in *X's & O's* to make a good assistant.

Jim never played high school basketball, so most of what he knows about the game he learned coaching on our staff at Hoover—and there's something to be said for that. If an assistant coach's basketball acumen is limited to the things he's been taught in *my* program, it guarantees that he will be teaching the things *I* have shown him to be important. I *do* think it's important to have some coaches on staff who bring a higher understanding of the game, as well, but it is not a prerequisite for every assistant I hire.

Jim also organizes the *Middle School Night*—a home date where all middle school players are introduced at halftime during one of our varsity games. This gives the players at the middle school a sense of attachment to the varsity program and it gets their parents into the varsity gym to see what a varsity game is like. This is especially big if they have never been to see a varsity game at Hoover. Again, connecting every level of the program to the whole is critical, and I try to involve as many people as I can at every level. Jim York is a big help to the program in this area.

Rounding out the high school staff, a huge addition at Hoover in the past few years, is a solid coach and a name many people will recognize—Todd Blackledge. Todd is a North Canton Hoover High School graduate who went to *Penn State* where he became the quarterback of the 1986 *National Championship* team, then went on to have a solid career in the *NFL* with the *Kansas City Chiefs* and *Pittsburgh Steelers*. However, Todd may be best known nation-wide today as a college football analyst, as he has become a broadcasting star in his role on *ESPN* and *ABC's* college football broadcasts. *Todd's Taste of the Town*—a segment where the cameras follow Todd into a different *local* restaurant each week to sample the cuisines unique to different regions of the country—has elevated his broadcasting career to *star* status.

My relationship with Todd started when he called to congratulate me when I accepted the job at Hoover. Two years later I asked him to join my staff, so he took over the freshmen team with his former high school friend and teammate, Paul Erikson. Paul is also a tremendous asset to my staff and he gives Todd flexibility until his season as a broadcaster ends in January.

Beyond coaching his ninth graders, Todd also works with our junior varsity and varsity players when time permits. I want Todd Blackledge doing as much as *he* wants to do for our program, so he sits on the bench with us on game nights, and I encourage him to use his keen ability to analyze everything we are doing in our program—the same ability he uses to analyze college football games on television.

Having Todd Blackledge on staff is a luxury. He brings a certain level of integrity to our program through his stature, through his reputation as being a quality person, and through his historical connection to the North Canton community. I am blessed to have Todd Blackledge on my staff.

Another critical aspect of a coaching staff is the middle school staff. At Hoover, we have four good ones—two at the eighth grade level who are *really* into it, Lance Graham and Kevin Stingel. Besides doing a terrific job coaching their eighth graders, they travel with us in the summer and help coach the varsity team in shootouts and team camp settings. This is a tremendous help, because the days a middle school coach coaches in the summer do not count against the ten days that the

Ohio High School Athletic Association allots a high school staff during the months of June and July. Having middle school assistants willing to go the extra mile allows me to put together an extensive summer program for the varsity team.

To go with some of the assistants I have already mentioned, John Kastor and Phil Johnson coach our seventh grade teams and both have made their best effort to learn the philosophy of our program. That said, because I only have so much time in my day, I have given my junior varsity coach, Jim York, the extra title of *Middle School Coordinator*. Whereas the entire staff tries to attend as many of the middle school games as possible, Jim attends almost all of them as my *middle school coordinator* so that he can help me keep my finger on the pulse of the young players in our program. Jim York works tirelessly and has *no* ego. He has evolved into a great coach—one that is very valuable to our program.

One other important role my middle school staff plays is the role of advance scouting. Scouting serves two purposes: it allows the coaches of the lower levels to learn more about the game, and its primary purpose is to help us learn about one of our upcoming opponents. I have one simple rule when it comes to scouting and hiring assistants: *If they don't want to scout, I don't hire them.*

Finally, one last critical piece to the staff is our *Elementary Coordinator*, Terry Cook. Terry was with me at Triway for 20 years. After a couple of years, Terry finally decided to come to Hoover with me, and I knew another huge piece to the staff puzzle was in place.

I often call Terry *The Director of Basketball Operations*, because he is so vital to the long-term success of the program. I give him my support whenever I am needed, but he is outstanding in getting the ball rolling with all aspects of our youth program at Hoover.

Truth be told, Terry Cook does so many things for the program I could devote an entire chapter to his work. Over the years he has secured major sponsors for the program, traveled on team trips, attended the state *Final Four* with the team, run the elementary league—complete with draft—and the list goes on and on. Terry is a very close friend and someone that every coach *needs* in his program.

Terry Cook is *exceptional*, but I believe there are people out there like him in every community. I believe it is vital for a head coach to find *a Terry Cook*, give him a role, and then simply sit back and watch him take things to great heights.

Former *UNLV* coaching legend Jerry Tarkanian—who spoke at our tip-off dinner one year at Hoover—told me he asked prospective assistants three simple questions, and if they answered 'yes' to any of them, he didn't even consider hiring them: *Do you fish? Do you play golf? Do you own a camper?* Tark told me a *'yes'* answer to any meant the prospective assistant had other interests in life and good coaches often *don't*. Simple as that for Tark, one of the truly colorful characters the coaching profession has known.

Now, I'm not sure we have the luxury as high school coaches to use Tark's criteria, but picking assistant coaches is extremely important, and it must be done with great care. When an assistant is chosen, he becomes a part of the inner circle—a concept that should not be taken lightly.

Best advice: Go slowly in picking a staff; if a former player is available that fits the bill, hire him, because he already knows you at your *best* and *worst* moments, and he *believes* in *your best-laid plans*. If a former player is not available, do your homework on the people that are available before bringing them in, because your assistants can make or break you.

100 (Kramer)

How important are assistant coaches to the success of a head coach? Consider the following hypothetical scenario:

You got fired after only three seasons—blindsided right in the middle of a rebuilding project that had started to show some real promise. Days pass, and while your several loyal assistants reach out to try to help you through the shock and pain, four of your assistant coaches don't so much as call or email—not to see how you're doing, not to thank you for the opportunity—nothing.

Within two days, Assistant-A has submitted his resume for the open position—before it has even been posted within the district. Meanwhile, Assistant-B—Assistant-A's buddy—is in the online 'chat rooms' and out in the community openly campaigning for his pal, telling anyone who will listen the things you did wrong and how much better things will be if his buddy is hired.

Assistant-C—inside of two weeks of your firing—has accepted a spot on the committee to interview and search for your successor. Assistant-D—who knows? He must have just been too busy to bother.

What inference can be drawn from the situation that was described? The head coach who was fired did a poor job of hiring a coaching staff. Furthermore, he knew those assistants were killing him two seasons prior to his firing, because he had witnessed great assistants up close in his former job and he just *knew* what he was witnessing with *this* staff wasn't right. Yet he *chose* not to do anything about it. Why?

Maybe the assistants *came with the program* when he accepted the job; maybe they were likable people; maybe there would have been political fall-out had he fired one or two of them; or maybe he just couldn't cope with the controversy that goes with firing an assistant coach. Whatever the case may have been, he chose not to fire them—so *he* got fired.

Would firing those four coaches have saved his job? Nobody will ever know. Perhaps they were just one piece of a very complex problem. But you can bet they sure didn't help. A coach's job is difficult enough without adding a group of assistants like that to the mix.

What's the best way for a coach to avoid the scenario I described? You would think experience. But ironically, experience taught *me* nothing—because I had the best coaching staff a high school head coach could ever hope to have in my final two years at Fairless, and I never took the time to reflect on how I assembled that staff—that is, until I *became* the head coach in the hypothetical scenario at the beginning of this section.

After looking back at one grandiose success and one staggering failure in choosing assistant coaches, I have come up with some *guidelines* that may be helpful to others in selecting a coaching staff.

Guideline #1: *Make sure you like the person before you hire him as your assistant.*

Every head coach says that *loyalty* is the number one quality desired in an assistant coach; I agree. The problem is, *loyalty* is something that cannot be *determined* in an interview—it's something that *must be proven* over a period of time. Of course, hiring *qualified* friends to fill every position would allow a head coach to bypass the effort it takes to build a loyal staff, but that's not a *reasonable* option for most coaches, *especially* coaches in their first head-coaching jobs. So, I believe the word '*like*' is key—without it, '*loyal*' isn't even a possibility.

What do I mean? Well, how many people are you truly *loyal* to that you don't—first—*like*? I'm not asking you how many bosses you worked for that you didn't like—that's a different question. I worked a union construction job for several companies in Cleveland to pay my way through my last two years of college at *Mount Union*, and I was a good employee. I liked some bosses; some I found to be obnoxious. But I'm quite certain I would *not* have jumped in front of an oncoming cement truck for any of them. I went to the construction site every day because I was loyal to my paycheck—not my bosses.

An assistant coach has to be more than a good employee. If you don't feel like you have a chance to be at least *professional friends* with the person, do not hire him to be an assistant coach. I'm not talking about someone who goes on vacation with your family every year or invites you to be in his wedding—although strong friendships do often blossom between coaches on a staff. I'm talking about hiring a person who is willing to go out to get a bite to eat with you before or after a game, a person who *wants* to scout games with you, a person who will sit with you and talk about the team—someone who is *not* always in a hurry to get out of the office and go home. How would one go about determining these things in an interview?

I would suggest an informal interview—over wings and a beer or even on the golf course—to allow the person to show his true personality. No interview will tell everything there is to know about a person, but an informal setting will reveal whether or not there is a basic compatibility. From there—like with any new friendship—time will tell.

> ***Guideline #2:** After a year on your staff, if the assistant has shown no signs of wanting to be a part of your basketball family beyond the time spent on the floor with the team, find someone to replace him.*

This may sound harsh, but I believe it's important for a coaching staff to grow together in much the same way players on a team need to grow together. I don't think it's possible to have a *quality* coaching staff unless solid relationships form.

When I took my first head-coaching job at Fairless in August of 2000, two assistants who had worked for my predecessor wanted to coach on my staff. They had no inherent loyalty *to me*, but they were both Fairless graduates who had coached in the program for several years; thus, they *seemed* very loyal *to the program*—which brings me to my third guideline.

> ***Guideline #3:** When accepting a new job, make sure to give those who were already there a chance to fit in on your new staff. Pushing aside qualified coaches who*

*were holdovers from the previous staff—especially if
they are respected members of the school community—
would be a huge public relations mistake.*

So, I interviewed both of them and I *liked* them—I felt each one had
the type of personality that could work well with me, and I was sure
each would want to do what was best for the Fairless program.

After a year on my staff, only one remained—a man by the name of
Eric Johnson. Coach Johnson was a terrific math teacher and a 1987
graduate of Fairless High School. We were the same age and, whereas
we had far different personalities, we had many similar interests off the
floor. Eric gave me three quality years as my varsity assistant; he was
loyal to me throughout—and he continued to be loyal to me when he
stepped away from coaching to become an assistant principal at Fairless. I was lucky to inherit Eric Johnson, a *life-long Fairless man*, when I
got the job at Fairless, and he is still a good friend of mine today—a
person with whom I regularly golf, play cards and socialize.

As for the other coach, he truly *believed* he was doing what was best
for Fairless. But he was *not* on board with the way *I* wanted things
done. He had played for a former Fairless coach who had utilized a far
different system of play, and he decided he wanted to coach that system,
not mine. He was not a bad person or even a bad coach, but he was not
loyal *to me*, the head coach, so we mutually decided at the end of my
first season that he would move on.

Both of the holdovers passed the first guideline by being likable
people in their interviews. After one year, Eric Johnson had become a
loyal friend and trusted assistant; the other coach decided he wanted to
do things his own way, and that put a strain on my relationship with
him that I neither needed nor had the time to fix. With one position
open heading into my second year, my staff would undergo its first
phase of evolution.

*Guideline #4: Have discussions with your coaches after
each season to see where they stand and be willing to
shuffle them into different positions to put them and
the staff in the best position to succeed.*

In a discussion with my junior varsity coach, Jeff Rollyson, right
after my first season, he informed me that he wanted to move into the
seventh-grade job that had opened. I liked Jeff at the junior varsity level
for a couple of reasons: first, we had been friendly foes on the blacktops

and in gyms in the Akron area growing up, so I *liked* him going in and suspected we would become friends. Second, Jeff had played sports at a high level—he was a very good high school baseball and basketball player at Akron Ellet who went on to play *baseball* at the University of Akron before being drafted by the Los Angeles Dodgers. When his impressive career in professional baseball stalled and ended at the Triple-A level, he decided to use his college degree to teach physical education and become the head baseball coach at Fairless High School.

Like Todd Blackledge on Coach Montgomery's staff, Jeff brought unique things to my staff because of *his* experience as a professional athlete. Plus, over the course of our first year together—as I suspected—he became a loyal friend. I didn't *want* to move him, but I also understood that he wanted to cut back on his responsibility to the basketball program so that he could transition to his role as head baseball coach sooner—the middle school basketball season typically ends in early February whereas the varsity season can overlap the beginning of baseball season by going well into March.

After listening to Jeff and taking some time to think it through, I realized granting his request would serve two purposes: first, it would allow me to keep a great asset to the program on board. Jeff had, in fact, become a *loyal* friend to me, and I knew he would do a top-notch job of working with me to make sure the middle school program was following *my* plan. Second, granting his request also opened up the junior varsity position for a hard-charging *basketball* coach who related well with the players and had a deep understanding of the *X's and O's*— a future head coach in the making.

Guideline #5: Hire family members only if they are highly qualified, and only if the timing is right.

I like my junior varsity coach to be someone who aspires to be a head coach—someone who will treat his junior varsity season as though he were coaching the *Los Angeles Lakers*. Steve Kramer—my brother three years younger—was the perfect fit.

Why didn't I hire him my first year? Hiring a relative is a tricky thing, so timing is important. I didn't think it would have been fair to Steve or me to hire him my first year and have him displace people who had been with the program for several years.

Since a coach left the program and Jeff Rollyson chose to move into the middle-school position, a perfect opportunity arose to hire Steve to fill the junior varsity position. I knew any program would be lucky to have a person as qualified as my brother at the junior varsity level, so I would have been a fool *not* to hire him.

Furthermore, my bosses at Fairless had watched me run my program for a year and trusted that I knew what I was doing. I assured them that Steve Kramer was going to be a tremendous asset to our program—so I hired him.

> *Guideline #6: Not every assistant coach has to be great with X's & O's, but it would be nice if at least one upper-level assistant brought that quality to the table.*

Steve Kramer was as good with *X's & O's* as any coach I have ever met. He was helpful on both ends of the court, but he was especially creative with offense. In the game of basketball, set plays and offensive continuity go in and out of style like the latest fads in clothing. But the concepts that Steve brought to my system—especially the screening and cutting action he developed to attack zones—have withstood the test of time and helped my teams win a number of games over the years.

I was fortunate enough to coach with my brother for four seasons before his life path took him in another direction—Steve began earning his teaching degree in his thirties and he simply came to a point where he had to commit full time to finishing it up. He was a tremendous coach, and fiercely loyal to me—and he loved the Fairless program and the players in it. When we got over the hump and made it to the *"Sweet-16"* in 2007, the work Steve had done with those players when they were freshmen and sophomores was a big reason why.

> *Guideline #7: If a position opens and a qualified candidate with strong community ties is available, hire him.*

When my brother left the staff at the end of the 2005 season, the final evolutionary phase of my staff at Fairless was set in motion. I felt we had gotten through the tough part of the rebuilding process, and a great chemistry had developed in our program. I didn't want to bring in an outsider—I wanted someone from inside the basketball family to fill the junior varsity job—so I looked to promote a coach from one of the lower levels of the program.

At the seventh-grade level I had Josh Witting, a young *aspiring* head coach and a 1998 Fairless graduate—from a *very* respected family in the community. Josh had spent two seasons as my seventh-grade coach and he had done a great job. But it was his *initiative* that made me decide to offer him the promotion.

The two years he coached at the seventh-grade level, when Josh wasn't coaching his own team, he was in the gym with the varsity team helping me. When his seventh-grade season ended in 2005, Josh approached me about coming to the varsity practices to help every day. I told him I would *love* to have him, and I offered him the opportunity to start sitting on the junior varsity and varsity benches on game nights—*nothing* did I ever appreciate more as a head coach than an assistant who wanted to do more.

Josh gratefully accepted the offer, and spent the final six games of the 2005 season with the high school staff. He did a number of things to help me that year, but the most important thing that happened was that our players became accustomed to seeing him and hearing his voice. He had become a *closer* member of the basketball family and he had shown me tremendous *loyalty* and the type of *work ethic* any head coach would want in an assistant. Whereas I knew I had lost one asset when my brother left, I was also certain the staff had gained another one—albeit with different qualities—when I promoted Josh to junior varsity coach.

> **Guideline #8: When someone becomes available who is already a loyal friend and understands sports and teaching kids, hire him—even if he knows nothing about basketball.**

Backtracking a bit, I hired my long-time best friend, Chris Lapish, to be my varsity assistant after the 2002 season when Eric Johnson left to become an assistant principal. Lape—as everyone called him—was a baseball, football and hockey player growing up in Romeo, Michigan, and never played a second of organized basketball in his life. In fact, his claim to fame—the one that made him an instant hit with the players and students—was the fact that he played *little league baseball* on the same team as his good friend, Bob Ritchie, better known to *the entire world* as *Kid Rock*.

Following his childhood brush with stardom, *we* became friends when we played travel softball together for a team out of Youngstown called *Mugsy's* in the early 1990's. At the time we met, I was about to graduate from *Mount Union College* with a teaching degree, and he was finishing up a sports management degree from Bowling Green that would land him a job at *IMG* in the motor sports division. Although our lives were traveling different routes, we remained friends over the years.

As time wore on—unhappy with the progress of his career at IMG—Lape went back to school and earned his teaching certificate. In the summer of 2002, he was searching for a job as a history teacher, and I was searching for a varsity assistant—and there was a history job open at Fairless High School.

The administration at Fairless honored my request to grant my good friend, Chris Lapish, an interview; two days later he accepted a teaching position, and he became my assistant coach. How could I hire an assistant coach who knew nothing about the game of basketball? Four reasons: I knew he was going to be fiercely loyal to me because we were best friends; I knew he was a bright sports mind who would pick things up quickly as I taught him; I knew he brought real-world organizational skills from his time at IMG that would make him great at handling some of the administrative things in the program; and most importantly, I *knew* my players would *love* him.

Sure enough, Chris Lapish was a great assistant coach to me for four years. But I knew he went into teaching with the idea that someday he would follow in *his* dad's footsteps—like I did with *my* dad.

Lape's dad was Michigan High School Baseball Hall-of-Fame Coach John Lapish—the man the baseball field at *Romeo High School* is named after. When Lape—you have to understand that *nobody* calls him Chris—accepted the job as the head baseball coach in August of 2006, he felt like it would be unfair to his new baseball program and to me to continue as my varsity assistant.

Knowing all too well the time commitments of a head coach, I understood, but I didn't want to *completely* lose him. *Coach* Lape had been a part of the *Fairless Basketball Family* for four years and stuck with it through a rebuilding phase; I wanted him to be around for the good times that I felt were coming—plus he had done a *professional* job of keeping our statistics updated in the local newspapers and promoting our players while helping organize our winter youth basketball organization.

Coach Lape had essentially become our *coordinator of basketball operations*—plus I loved having such a close friend on my staff—so I offered him the chance to stay on in *that* role. He accepted—meaning he would continue with his off-the-floor duties and still sit on the bench on game nights. This created a best-case scenario for me, because we kept a valuable member of the coaching staff on board—at almost no cost—*and* opened a spot to hire another assistant *basketball* coach.

Guideline #9: If you can get a former head coach on your staff that would be happy being your assistant, hire him.

Tim Vick never wanted to coach boys' basketball; he played for legendary Stark County coach Larry Wilson at Perry High School, and he cut his coaching teeth in the girls program under Margaret Peters at Jackson High School.

In 1999, Coach Vick accepted the head girls' job at Fairless and his seven-year tenure makes him worthy of being considered *the* most successful girls' coach in the history of Fairless High School.

After a four-year run that produced a ninety percent victory rate, two league titles, a District Championship and "*Sweet-16*" appearance, he resigned his post as the head girls' coach. In our time together sharing a gym as head basketball coaches, each of us had gained a respect for the job the other was doing running a program. In that time, we shared ideas, confided in each other and became the best of friends off the floor.

After Tim resigned, he told me he needed some time away to recharge his battery. I watched up close how hard Tim charged in leading an unprecedented run of success of Fairless girls' basketball, and I knew he stepped away from the helm because he was physically and emotionally exhausted from all the things that a *head-coaching job* includes, *mostly* off the floor. So when Chris Lapish vacated the varsity assistant's job on *my* staff, I approached Tim—in a light-hearted manner—about being my associate head coach.

At first Tim scoffed at the idea and we *both* laughed it off as being a far-fetched scenario. I would have actually been fine if he had never sincerely considered my offer—but I knew I had planted a seed. I knew Tim loved the game, and I thought he might enjoy coaching *without* the added stress of being the head coach. So, I let it sit with him and never mentioned it again.

A week later, with the start of the school year casting its shadow on August, Tim told me he would consider joining my staff—if I were willing to allow him to do more than just hold the clipboard. Done deal: I told him that he would be my *associate head coach*. I guaranteed Tim that I would give him full authority to use his expertise in teaching his vaunted man-to-man defense, and I told him I'd even let him take an equal share of the blame for the losses if it would make him feel of greater value. Tim accepted all but that last bit of the offer, filling a two-year void on my staff created when my brother Steve left after the 2004-05 season.

Tim Vick brought an assistant with an expert's basketball acumen back to my staff—his specialty being on the defensive end of the court. I felt that Tim's defensive package would complement my offensive system perfectly to create the up-tempo game I wanted our skilled, guard-oriented team to play—so another piece of the puzzle to building the ideal coaching staff was in place.

Guideline #10: The Todd Blackledge rule: When good fortune hands you a perfect addition to your staff from an unlikely place, find a spot for him.

To build a great coaching staff requires good decision-making, the ability to adapt and, frankly, some old-fashion good luck. The likelihood of finding *a Todd Blackledge*—*a* former *NFL* quarterback and current *ESPN* college football analyst who also has a passion for coaching high school basketball—is not very high in most districts. Coach Montgomery is great at a lot of things—that's just plain lucky.

Well, I didn't find a television personality, but I got just as lucky when good fortune sent me the Reverend Mike Husted. At 6'9" and the father of an *NCAA Division-II All-American*—Jeff Husted from *Gannon University*—Coach Husted had *instant* credibility with his position group. Just as importantly, I knew Mike was a man of impeccable moral fiber who would bring a minister's perspective to the locker room

I watched Mike *teach* my *big kids* at Fairless—none of whom were taller than 6'3"—to make significant contributions to the guard-laden teams we had that were so successful during the 2006-07 and 2007-08 seasons. But the thing I remember most about Mike's influence on my players is a scene frozen in my mind that took place prior to our *Regional Semi-final* game on March 15th of 2007 at the *Canton Memorial Civic Center:*

I was hypnotized by both the gravity of the moment and the nostalgia brought on by remembering the joy I took in growing up a coach's kid. As I panned the arena in awe of the more than thirty-five hundred people from *our* rural community who had dressed in blue and silver, and assembled beneath the bright lights of the downtown arena to witness *Fairless'* third-ever appearance in a *"Sweet-16,"* my memory pressed the button that said 1977—and my mind's eye was racing through my first trip to the *Canton Civic Center,* the night I watched my dad's Hoban team play in a regional...

Driving up to the bright lights outside the arena; the winding path into the parking deck; walking amongst the electric crowd from the city street into the arena through one of hundreds of reflective glass doors and seeing the lines of people at the box offices; pushing through the turnstile and through the waves of fans, then past the concession stand and the smell of popcorn in the bowels of the stadium, and finding the tunnel whose light at the other end exploded into my first look at the big time—Broadway lighting bouncing off of every perfectly placed board of the raised court, the pro-style basket standards that sat at both ends of the floor, the sky box that hung at the top of the arena on both sides, the usher to whom I handed my ticket so he could help me find my place in a sea of cushioned theatre seats that stretched the length of both sides of the court and looped around one end zone to create a horseshoe. Was this really a high school basketball game? It was Madison Square Garden in downtown Canton, and I knew that night—before I had been on earth for a decade—that I wanted to be a participant in the Canton Civic Center some-day.

As the roar of the crowd watching the game before ours reminded me 'someday' had arrived, my eight-year-old eyes aged thirty years, shrinking the arena's size by two-thirds. Back in the moment, I realized the hazy lighting created a setting that looked like it could have been clipped right out of a classic *ABA* reel from the 1970's. I half expected to see fans start to light up their cigars and cigarettes and my players to put on their gold chains, when I caught *classic Mike Husted* at work out of my peripheral vision.

With over five-thousand fans in the stands and the commotion of a frantic finish to a one-point game unfolding in front us, the four post players—kids we would need to play well if we were to have *any* chance against a much bigger, much more athletic Cleveland Benedictine team—stood at attention around Coach Husted while he reviewed their assignments. And they were *100%* focused—in a way teachers and coaches can only *dream* of. Then *the minister* in Mike offered them a short blessing, and they each hugged him as the buzzer sounded telling us it was time to take the floor for warm-ups…

Watching Mike focus his post players ended my detour on memory lane and snapped me back into the moment. But it also made me real-ize what a *truly* special person Mike Husted *is* and how much he meant to my coaching staff. The way my post players at Fairless migrated toward Mike prior to games—the way they listened to him and tried to please him—was picture-perfect coaching.

I felt that adding Mike Husted made my staff as complete a staff as I could have ever imagined. We had it *all* covered, *even* the spiritual world—we joked as a staff that with "Minister Mike" sitting next to Tim Vick we had *God's* influence and *The Devil's* sitting on our bench. Of course, I imagine God had bigger things on His plate most nights than to care one way or the other whether or not Fairless won its basketball game; however, I bet He was very pleased with the mentoring my players were getting from Mike and the rest of the staff—a staff that was truly *special*.

The point: *Special* people create *special* moments. Josh Witting, my junior varsity coach and a head coach in the making; my associate head coach and defensive coordinator, Tim Vick; Mike Husted, my post specialist, the team minister and my personal spiritual advisor; my longtime best friend, Chris Lapish—my former varsity assistant who was still with us on game nights in charge of statistics and media relations. The only person missing was my brother Steve Kramer, who sat in the stands during our magical run to a *"Sweet-16"* in 2007, realizing the players and coaches considered him a card-carrying member of our basketball family. Seven years to achieve *special*.

Why does it take so long? Because true friendships and solid relationships are not built overnight. These men were *great* for the program and *great* for the kids, but most of all, these men all became the best friends I have in the world. That's what made it more than a successful basketball staff—the friendships are what *made* it *special*.

Like Coach Montgomery said in his section, *assistant coaches can either make or break a head coach*. My hope is that the guidelines I carved out of the process that led to building the *special* staff that helped *'make me'* at Fairless will show other coaches the *care* it takes to build their own special staffs—and avoid the staff that helped break *the coach* in the *hypothetical situation* I used in my introduction of this section.

7

Promoting the Program:

Internally & Externally

500

AS LEADERS, WE work so hard to coach our kids, and that is certainly a key aspect of the job. However, I have always believed that it is also important to take more of a *college approach* to promoting a program. With all of the technology available today, creating exposure for a basketball program is not a difficult thing to do. Over the years, with the help of those around me, I have done many things to promote and expose my programs at Triway and Hoover to the outside.

The most obvious way to get program promotion underway is through *the web*. Not that this is a novel idea, because I'm sure many programs are doing this, but we have always had a program website that can be used as a source of information for those interested in our program. On our website at Hoover, we include things that range from our schedule and game results, to camp registrations, and general program points of interest. We have also recently added links that allow viewers to log into the websites of the college basketball programs where our former players are playing. The longer the website exists, the more we update it and add things to it so that it is an ever-evolving source of information on Hoover basketball.

Another great source of promotion for us has been our basketball-specific media guide. This media guide—an idea I stole from *Bob Huggins* when I was working as his assistant at *Walsh College* back in the early 1980's—is separate from the regular program that all booster clubs make available to the public.

The first thing Bob Huggins did for promotion at *Walsh College* when he got the job was make a press guide that was one of the best in the country. The average fan or coach might wonder if anyone cares enough about his program to go to those lengths to create such a press guide, but that's missing the point. The press guide is another way of *making* people care.

That first press guide Bob created at *Walsh* had everything from bios on the players to a full-color front cover—very rare and expensive *in 1980.* With the help of Steve Burgess, who was Walsh's resident genius with promotional matters, Bob Huggins spared no expense to make the media guide something that set the Walsh program apart from others.

Of course the media guide was a great way to get information out to the public about the program, but it had other merits beyond that— the biggest being that it was a great recruiting tool. The media guide was something we could give to recruits and their parents that showed the kids we were really committed to getting the best available players to come to Walsh.

Obviously, public high schools do not recruit players from around the country, but they do need to recruit kids within their school systems to participate in their programs—and this goes for any public school sport or organization. I have already stressed the importance that I place on connecting all levels of the program to keep interest high, and the media guide is another quality thing that makes kids in our school district say, *"I want to be a Hoover Viking basketball player someday."*

Hoover is not the only high school that has taken the concept of the media guide to a higher level. *Moeller High School* in Cincinnati has the best Media Guide I have ever seen; in fact, it is every bit as nice as Ohio State's. *Karl Kremer,* Moeller's head coach, does a great job in establishing a first-class program. Their book is all color and includes information that is both steeped deeply in the tradition and history of Moeller basketball and highly informative when it comes to the current Moeller players. At Hoover, our media guide holds to a similar concept, and although it is not yet as good as Moeller's, we strive every year to make it the best it can possibly be.

We use our media guide to get information out to the press, to the parents, our fans, future Hoover Viking players and visiting fans. We also have found it to be quite useful in exposing our players to college coaches who may be interested in recruiting them. The media guide has become a staple for my programs over the years, and I would highly recommend to any coach who does not yet have one in place to begin developing a media guide for his program *right now.*

I could go on and on about program promotion, because I have tried a number of things at Triway and Hoover over my twenty-plus years in coaching, but there are three more things that I'd like to share that have either been great promotions in the past or are currently annual events on our basketball calendar. One major event that has become an annual event at Hoover is our *Tip-off Dinner*.

The *Tip-off Dinner* does just what is says—it tips off the season in a positive way for our basketball community in North Canton—and it has proven to also be a great moneymaker for our program. The dinner is a formal affair with a first-class meal and a silent auction that usually provides some very nice sports-related items; also, we have always been fortunate to have a keynote speaker at the dinner that has celebrity status in the sporting world.

Past speakers have been former *Cy Young Award winner* Dean Chance; former *Cleveland Indians* manager and current manager of the *Philadelphia Phillies*, Charlie Manuel; former *Boston Celtic* Larry Siegfried; former *Cleveland Cavalier* star Larry Nance; *NFL* coach and former head college football coach Ron Blackledge; Dick Snyder, a former *NBA* player and Hoover great; and the former *National Championship* coach from *UNLV* Jerry Tarkanian. The Tip-off Dinner, featuring our keynote speakers, have provided a great way of getting the season off to an exciting start, and it's another way of promoting *Hoover* as a *first-class basketball organization*.

Another event that has become annual at Hoover is the showcase we run over Martin Luther King weekend now called *The Mercy Medical Classic*. The Classic is run first class all the way and it brings some of the best high school programs in the State of Ohio, and beyond, to Stark County each January.

It takes great leadership to start an event like The Mercy Medical Classic. Three highly successful local businessmen—Gene DeChellis, Greg Duplin and Charlie Oberholzer—have chaired The Classic and they have been the backbone of the year-round planning that running an event of this magnitude requires.

Our goal in running The Mercy Medical Classic is to offer local basketball fans a buffet of intriguing match-ups to watch over the long weekend while providing a first-class experience for all of the programs involved. We get things started each year the Monday prior to the event with a pre-Classic press conference at a local country club. At the press conference there is local radio, television and newspaper coverage, and each team is invited to bring its staff and two or three of its players to enjoy a catered meal and interact with the media. The press conference has been a great way to tip off a week of great competition and good sportsmanship.

On game day, when the teams arrive at our facility, a host meets them and stays with them until their evening ends. Each player receives an event t-shirt, and the coaches receive event golf shirts and a briefcase with the event logo on it. And every member of each team's traveling party receives a catered Italian meal following their game.

Of course at the center of it all is the competition. My top assistant, Troy Clark, does a great job of putting the match-ups together every year so that the games will draw crowds and create an atmosphere that will begin to prepare the participants and fans for the tournament season. We sell single-game tickets, daily passes and passes that are good for the entire weekend—and it has been a good source of fund-raising for our program, because the event draws well.

The event offers great exposure for Hoover, certainly, but it also offers great exposure for every school that participates. Besides the press conference, there is also a top-notch media guide we offer—which is not only a nice keepsake for the participants, but also a first-class way for the many college coaches who are in attendance to track the players of interest from each school.

Like I said, it takes great leadership to put all of this together year in and year out, and none of it would be possible without quality men like Gene, Charlie and Greg who brought successful business experience and made The Mercy Medical Classic one of the finest events anywhere—and another great promotion for my program at Hoover.

Looking into the past, another huge moneymaker that became a community event on an annual basis when I was at Triway was the *3-on-3 Tournament* we held each summer. This *3-on-3 Basketball Extravaganza* was a spectacle that went well beyond the games being played and, in fact, really became a weekend event each summer that generated a *festival* atmosphere in the area surrounding Wooster, Ohio. We had a circus tent, carnival games, hot air balloons, and just about any type of concessions a hungry or thirsty patron's taste buds could desire—and kids from several different states came to participate in the tournament.

Most of the games were played on Kiper Courts—an outdoor facility at Triway named after the late Mark Kiper, a former player of mine who was tragically killed in a roadside accident. Mark Kiper's dad, Charlie, and mom, Joan, were also major supporters of the 3-on-3

Tournament, and continued to be active in helping the program for the duration of my time at Triway. Events like this not only raise money and promote the program to the public, but they also expand and strengthen the inner circle by getting great people involved.

At Triway, this event actually became so big after its fifth year that we were able to secure a major *$10,000* sponsorship from a local car dealership and the *Rubbermaid Company* based in Wooster, Ohio. Running an event of this magnitude was certainly a ton of work, but it was a labor of love—and the labor we put in paid off exponentially in fun and finances while galvanizing the entire community *in the name of Triway basketball.*

Over the years I certainly have done a number of other smaller things to promote the program—things that I am sure I didn't invent. I have always done schedule cards with the pictures of the program's seniors on them; I always have a billboard in our community that displays a promotion for our upcoming season; and my varsity players throw t-shirts into the crowd during introductions at our home games. If there's one thing I have learned over the years it is that *no* promotional act is so small that it goes unnoticed.

With that in mind, I believe that a coach must really work at providing a positive image for his program in his own community and the basketball community at large. Through the technology we have available in this day and age, high school sports have become a huge source of entertainment that transcend the boundaries of their regularly scheduled seasons. To me, the better programs let their communities know they are there year-round by providing promotional events that allow the members of the community to form deeper connections to those programs.

100 (Kramer)

Since Coach Montgomery did a masterful job of sharing his ideas on promoting a program to the public, I'm going to provide a bit different perspective by talking about how I promote to those inside the program while going through the process of rebuilding...

Here's an aphorism about rebuilding which I live by: *Losing games is not a bad thing—as long as it serves as a means toward a successful future.*

When a coach is given the roster I had in 2003-04 at Fairless and again in 2010 at Canton South, he is going to lose *games*—and I lost a bunch of them. In 2004, at Fairless, my team went *3-19* with *seven* seniors getting a lion's share of the minutes; in 2005 it went *4-18* with four freshmen and three sophomores constructing seven of the top nine spots in the rotation; and in 2006, a year that we *did* enjoy the services of one pretty good senior—to go along with a group of underclassmen that were maturing nicely—we improved to *10-12*.

The process was steady, but slow, and the first time I went through it I was never *absolutely* sure I could lead Fairless to the top—at least not until the very moment I was standing on a ladder in the *Canton Memorial Field House* cutting a net down after we had won the *2007 Canton Division-II District Championship* against *two-time defending State Division-II Runner-up* Triway. At that moment, I felt confident I had found a pretty good method for rebuilding.

No magic, no miracles: It starts with *internal promotion*—or focusing on the things *within* the program that a coach *can* control to create a culture in which success is possible. It's a delicate process that takes time—perhaps years—and it also depends greatly on the support of a patient and understanding administration if it is to end happily.

The attitude of the head coach—the CEO of the program—is where it starts, so I'd like to start by suggesting one thing a coach should *not* do to internally promote his program: *play the blame game*. There is absolutely no reason to attempt to make it public knowledge that the former coach is to blame—doing so portrays a poor attitude right from the start.

The former coach very well may have been a good deal at fault for neglecting the program at one level or another. However, another possibility is that it was nobody's fault. Maybe there were simply a couple of classes of bad athletes in a row and no amount of effort or coaching could have changed a couple of tough seasons. Either way, what difference does it make?

Publicly blaming the former coach, rightfully so or not, is nothing more than a hollow effort at saving one's ego—an excuse to pawn off a tough season on someone else before that season ever starts. It's an effort that is likely to go ignored by the casual supporter and resented by those who have been staunch supporters of the program. Remember, the school hired a coach, not someone to assess blame—by taking the time to blame the former coach, time has been taken away from working to rebuild the program.

Another product of *playing the blame game* is that the new coach has started his tenure as the leader of his program by indirectly attacking the character and ability of every one of his upperclassmen, thus pushing an entire group of parents permanently on the defensive. Blaming is not just a bad idea, it's *the worst* possible thing a coach can do when taking over a program and trying to instill a new positive attitude.

So with blaming off the table as an option, there is no choice but to go to work and do what every coach is hired to do—*lead*. Coach Montgomery once told me, "*Sometimes leading means standing alone.*" There is no lonelier time as a head coach than when the program is struggling at the top. Therefore, once I realized winning games consistently was not going to be realistic for a period of a season or two, my first goal was to line up some allies that would stand loyally by me as the program went through the challenges of the rebuilding process. That's what leaders do, right?

Leaders sell people in their charge on a vision, build relationships, and get those people to follow *their best-laid plans*, to work hard, and to stay true to the task. Looking back to the situation at Fairless, finding my core people was *the key* to the entire operation. Therefore, when I recognized that a similar process was going to need to take place at Canton South, I was certain that it needed to start with finding my core people. Here's the key: knowing where to look to find *the right people* to *allow* into the inner circle.

When I'm looking for *my people*, I go straight to the level of the program that has the strongest basketball class and start my search right there. When we were rebuilding at Fairless in 2004, I had three really good freshmen that would play huge roles in our future success, but my strongest class in the program was my eighth-grade class. That class was eight kids deep with potential varsity players, and a couple of them were magnificently skilled. Making them even stronger, they were a close-knit group of friends who all loved the game of basketball—gym rats to an extreme degree—and it showed when they practiced and played.

Knowing their development was essential to the renaissance of my program, I watched those eighth graders as much as my schedule would let me—something as simple as that is how I started internally promoting my program. The players in that class saw me at their practices and their games on *almost* a daily basis. I wanted the kids in that class to understand that they were going to serve as the cornerstone of the rebuilding process, and I wanted to *empower* them to take *ownership* of the program as they were walking into the high school for the first time.

By being visible at those practices and games I not only forged strong relationships with the players at an early stage, but the parents of those players also got to know me on a positive level, and they became comfortable with me. Pretty soon a number of the parents of the kids at the eighth-grade level began asking me how they could get involved with the program to help out. That was the start of what was called the *"Basketball Moms Club"*—a club that actually consisted of basketball moms and dads.

The club became stronger and stronger under the leadership of the parents, many from that eighth-grade class of 2004, and they were doing amazing things for our players by the end of my stretch at Fairless. Whereas I was operating under a budget at Fairless that could give our kids all the necessities, the parents of our Basketball Moms Club provided our players with plenty of the extras that programs with much bigger budgets enjoy.

We had team meals; we stayed in nice hotels when we traveled in the summer; we took the players to amusement parks and major league baseball games on our summer trips; we ate in nice restaurants; and we took one really nice trip each summer to play in what most people would consider to be a *special* venue—the nicest being a four-day trip to Chapel Hill, North Carolina in 2008 to play twelve games in the *Dean Smith Center at the University of North Carolina*. With the help of the Basketball Moms Club, our program became something every boy growing up at Fairless wanted to be a part of.

I appreciated everything the Basketball Moms Club did for my program and our players. But the thing that I appreciated the most is that the parents in the club *supported* and *promoted* the program *externally* when we were going through our tough times at the varsity level—just like a family supports its members through difficult times.

A coach will always have detractors, but those detractors become more visible when the team struggles at the varsity level, because those struggles give the detractors an audience. None of that matters if the audience does not include those that directly affect the operation of the program. In fact, a strong group of parents who support the program can actually insulate the program from any negative energy that might be out there, and that's important, because a team and its players are most susceptible to negative outside influences when it is struggling the most.

At the height of our struggles, the player I worried about the most was a terrific young point guard by the name of Jonah Manack. Jonah probably had the toughest road to travel of any of our players during the rebuilding process at Fairless because—while his brother Garret was in eighth grade starring on an undefeated middle school team with his classmates—Jonah was a ninth grader starting at point guard for the 2003-04 varsity team that was winning *three* out of twenty-two games. The following year when those eighth graders became ninth graders and four of them were earning varsity letters, Jonah's sophomore year started with a big fat *0-12*.

In all, Jonah Manack started his high school basketball career by losing 31 of the first 34 games in which he played. I don't care how mentally tough a kid is, that kind of struggling will take a toll on him, and I worried about the toll the losing might be having on Jonah—until a conversation I had with Jonah's mom prior to our thirteenth game of Jonah's sophomore season.

Lori Manack, prominent leader of the Basketball Moms Club, told me before our thirteenth game of Jonah's sophomore year that she was amazed at how optimistic her two boys—Jonah and Garret—had remained through the difficult times. When I asked her what she meant, she told me that Jonah and Garret went into every game believing we had the right game plan to win. She told me her two boys trusted me unconditionally. That was huge! Here we were 0-12, and one of the key leaders of my parent group—mother of two key members of my rebuilding project—was spreading the positive word about the way I was running the program. I knew that if I had Lori and her husband, Gary Manack, on board at 0-12, the other parents would stay on board with them and positively promote the program, too.

More importantly, I knew those parents would promote a positive approach in their sons—the boys that I needed to continue to develop for us to become successful on game nights. I believe there's a message in there for all parents.

The night Lori Manack gave me that complement, we broke through and earned our first win of the 2004-05 season, and the rest of that season we played *.500* basketball. The following season, Jonah Manack's junior year, we won ten games and scored a huge tournament upset victory in the first round over a team that entered the game with a 17-3 record. Ten wins doesn't sound like much, but when you consider that a player like Jonah had endured a 3-31 stretch, it was huge to the program moving into the 2006-07 season—the year we felt like we might just be able to see some real payoff for the hard work we put into rebuilding.

As it turned out, the 2006-07 season did pay off big. On March 10th, 2007, in front of a crowd of over 4,000 fans at the *Canton Memorial Field*

House, I was privileged to coach the same boys who had been 0-12 just twenty-four months earlier to the *Canton D-II District Championship*, earning a trip to Fairless' third-ever "*Sweet-16*". As I stood there watching each of those young men climb the ladder and cut down the nets to cheers from the adoring Fairless community, I could not help but think that none of the great times we were experiencing could have been possible without the support and promotion given to the program by the parents of those young men.

Lori and Gary Manack; Deb and Carl Erb; Brenda and Jim Jennings; Therese and Jim Penland; and Lori and Dave Soehnlen are all charter members of what I deemed the *Parents' Club Hall of Fame*. Without their leadership and positive promotion of the program when times were tough, I'm not sure the rebuilding process would have been possible at Fairless, where the *basketball program* truly had become a *basketball family*.

When I left Fairless to return to my home community as the head coach at Canton South, I was in a similar situation to the one I confronted at Fairless in 2004. The varsity talent was thin—just like I was told it would be when I accepted the job the previous spring. I inherited just two legitimate varsity players—a solid shooting guard by the name of Matt Trissel and an ultra-athletic 6'2" wing named Jerald Robinson. I liked both kids and their potential to thrive in my system—if I could find some functional players to put around them.

Unfortunately, I quickly found there wasn't a whole lot of commitment to basketball beyond those two, which made it difficult to start implementing my system during the summer contact period. I knew I could fix the *lack-of-commitment* problem over time—just as I had at Fairless—but I couldn't do it in time to affect that first season at Canton South.

I spent the months following the summer season and leading up to our first practice wondering where I would find the players *to* put on the court with Matt Trissel and Jerald Robinson. There were a number of sophomores who had a chance to develop into *decent* players, but none of them were ready to log big varsity minutes—they just weren't. And to make matters worse, I lost a starter who could have been a pretty good player when he was expelled from school for—of all things—punching the resource officer in our building.

The thin talent pool, along with a general lack of commitment, plus some extra things—like punching a cop—opened the door for two transfers who were castoffs from other programs to come in and play as seniors. Both young men had some ability, but neither had played long enough to understand organized basketball. More importantly, neither had been around in the summer to start picking up on *my* system. But they were *clearly* two of the top five or six players in the gym so, under the circumstances, they deserved to play.

Of course, we were behind all of the established programs to begin with, and adding two players who were starting as blank slates set us back even further. It also made it impossible for anyone, including me, to put a finger on *any* expectations. I thought Matt Trissel and Jerald Robinson could play well, but the rest was a mystery.

As it turned out, Matt Trissel—the fourth all-time leader in passing yardage in the storied history of Stark County high school football— came right off the gridiron firing. He was my kind of player, making *fifty* three-point goals and putting up some twenty-point games. Jerald struggled to get his *basketball legs* early in the season, but came on to average just over twenty points and ten rebounds over the course of the last ten games. And thankfully we received some decent play out of the two transfers—so we *did* stay competitive.

In the end, my first team at Canton South won nine games and, whereas we really could have won a few more, most people felt it was a reasonable number for a team with no expectations and few returning players. I felt like that first season gave me a good starting point to continue to rebuild the South program, but I was also certain we were not going to be ready to make a run at the league championship or a district championship the next season, 2009-10.

The biggest reason I was *reasonably* optimistic about improvement heading into my second season at South was the development of Jerald Robinson. My first season at South, Jerald Robinson, as a junior, had become the type of player I felt could lead a young team in 2009-10 to another *competitive* season while my prized incoming ninth-grade class began to make contributions. I couldn't imagine what we would do without Jerald that next year, because I knew our junior varsity team had struggled and Jerald was the owner of all of our returning scoring, rebounds and assists. I envisioned Jerald Robinson as the guy who would protect my young players and show them how to compete at the varsity level. Yes, I thanked God for Jerald Robinson.

Well, in the spring of Jerald's junior year of high school, The University of Michigan offered him a football scholarship and the Wolverines coach at the time, Rich Rodriguez, felt it would be best if Jerald were to leave Canton South High School in January of his senior year to start taking college classes so he would be eligible for spring football. I was elated for Jerald to get such a prestigious opportunity, and when he asked me what I thought, I gave him my blessing.

Of course that meant Jerald would not be playing basketball for me his senior year. It also meant we would return *exactly zero points per game at the varsity level* in my second season at South—another reason for a person in Ohio to *hate* Michigan.

After spending a season teaching Jerald the skills he needed to become the centerpiece of the program, he was gone and we were left with a whole bunch of players who had never stepped foot on a varsity basketball floor. How many is a whole bunch?

With Jerald gone and *zero* returning varsity players, *thirty-seven* boys grades nine through twelve came to our first practice to open my second season at Canton South—*thirty-seven*. I felt like asking the art department if someone could paint *The Statue of Liberty* on our locker room door, because the word was out that the basketball program was the land of opportunity.

The best player in that group was clearly a 5'6" freshman point guard named Armand Fontes—a player that would have been *far* better served to complete a successful season of *winning* junior varsity games. Instead, Armand started every *varsity* game as a freshman.

The second best player was Mark Trissel, an athletic, undersized, left-handed post player and younger brother of Matt Trissel—the fine shooting guard who had graduated the previous year. I thought Mark and Armand could be decent varsity players—that wasn't the problem. The problem was that *number thirty-two* on the depth chart didn't look a whole lot different than *number three*—and *not* because we had great depth.

To be fair, *some* of the kids in that *rave* could do some things on the court; the difficult part was sorting them out and assigning them to a level. Every day someone new did something in practice that made me feel like I needed to give him an opportunity—so I did. But nobody ever had two practices in a row that stood out.

The more I watched practice, I became certain of what I had feared: we didn't have a *varsity* team. So I went back to my roots as a head coach at Fairless and decided that if we were going to start from scratch on the court—which invariably means losing games—then I would need to work overtime on *internal program promotion*.

94

Because of the similarities in the situation at South in 2009-10 to the one with which I was confronted in 2003-04 at Fairless, I felt confident in my methods. I don't think any two situations are ever going to be *exactly* the same, but I swear the basketball players who entered high school at Canton South for the 2009-10 season as freshman were the multi-cultural version of the ones that entered Fairless in 2004. They were tight-knit friends; they had a very good skill base as a group; and they were gym rats. When I watched this group play as eighth graders my first year at South as the head coach, I immediately thought they had a chance to be *special*, so I gave them the same attention that I had given my prize class at Fairless in hope that I'd get similar results with the buy-in by the kids and their parents.

After one year with them, I had become very close with the players, and relationships with their parents had turned into a support group. The program had not become a basketball family yet, but those bonds *were* forming.

When I took the head coaching job at Canton South, a parent group specific to the basketball program did *not* exist. I'm all for an athletic booster club, but I believe a basketball-specific organization must be in place if a program is going to be capable of giving the best of things to its players. Similarly to the way that it happened at Fairless, the more the parents became comfortable with me and saw the relationships I was building with their sons, the more they began to ask what they could do to help. Coaching is a *people* business, and I enjoy the relationships that can be built by getting people involved.

The summer prior to my third season at Canton South, four sets of parents had distinguished themselves as willing to help in any way possible—mostly transporting kids to shootouts and providing snacks and drinks for the road, and simply being there all the time. So after the summer schedule ended, I invited them to my house for a cookout to thank them for their time and help.

I wanted those parents to understand how much I appreciated their help—that was my only motive for the cookout. That said, as the evening wore on, one of the parents suggested that the basketball parents form a club *specifically* for the purpose of promoting and supporting the basketball program. Thus, the *Canton South Sideliners Club* was born.

The whole thing is so similar to the process at Fairless it makes me believe that there are good people in *every* community that are willing to help a hard-working coach make his program better for their sons.

The names were different at Canton South, but the parents there did the same type of things to help my program as those families I mentioned earlier did for the program at Fairless. What was the most important thing the parent group did?

Easily the most important thing they did was to provide a support group that vigorously promoted my program through a difficult twelve months on the varsity scoreboard. How difficult? Try 1-20 difficult. Think that opens the door for some potential negativity?

About right now, many readers are probably asking themselves the obvious question: *This guy went one 1-20 and he's writing a book?* Trust me when I say that the *1-20* season slowed down my enthusiasm for completing this project. Like so many things in coaching, it certainly made me question the things I was doing. However—ironically—I am *certain* the *3-19* and *1-20* seasons made this book more useful. How?

When the one-win season ended, I noticed some things that made me believe that maybe I was on to some ideas that could help other coaches experiencing a complete rebuild. First, I saw that my core kids—the ones that I believe will one day climb the same ladders my kids at Fairless climbed in 2007 to take down the nets at the Canton Field House—were one-hundred percent with me. Second, I also realized that I had a *bigger* parent support group at the end of that difficult year than I had before it started. The team had struggled on the scoreboard at the varsity level, but a *basketball family* had been born that would lay the foundation for future success.

I can say without question that forging positive relationships and building a strong inner circle for the basketball program is *the key* to the rebuilding process. Developing this strong inner circle is what I consider promoting my program *internally*. Once internal promotion has created a strong inner group, the natural progression will be that those on the inside will spread the positive word to the outside public. After a while, people who want to be negative will be without an audience, and the program will be able to develop at its own pace in a positive learning environment. It sounds like I'm oversimplifying, but I've seen all of this unfold in two different schools in two different communities, and I strongly believe internally promoting my program is where it all started.

One *caveat*: Rebuilding a program takes time—years—and none of the things I have suggested in this section matters if a coach's administration looks only at the scoreboard and never takes the time to investigate and see the strong relationships that have been built by getting the right kids in the locker room. In both of my positions as a head coach—Canton South and Fairless—I constructed and diligently applied *similar plans* to rebuild and promote my program.

At Fairless, I had an administration that took the time to look beyond game nights during the rebuilding years, get to know me and see the special things we were doing in our program. That's why my tenure at Fairless ended with my basketball family standing on ladders cutting down championship nets.

At Canton South, I had an administration—albeit not the one that hired me—that never came around except on game nights. They ultimately passed judgment on me solely based on a scoreboard that was a year away from yielding consistently happy endings. That's why my tenure at Canton South ended with me standing in front of fourteen sobbing basketball players—teenage boys who had come to see me as their mentor—telling them that *their* basketball family would have a new leader.

Sometimes *the best-laid plans* work to perfection, and sometimes they don't.

8

Daily Practice Rituals:

What do you want your team to be good at?

500 (Montgomery)

PRACTICE IS A place for the players to improve their individual skills; it is a place for the coaches to mesh the individual skills and talents of the players together; and it is a place for me to constantly evaluate the development of both the individual players and the team. All that considered, *the* most important aspect of any practice is the careful planning that goes into it so that *all* things important are covered and the team is consistently prepared. To insure individual and team development in the key areas, our sessions are structured so that certain drills and routines are a part of each and every practice, from the beginning to the end of the season.

First of all—in my opinion—any coach who does not include individual fundamentals in his daily practice plan is making a mistake. Basketball is a game of skill, which can only be created through the mastery of the game's fundamentals. I realize that a certain amount of time needs to be spent on preparing for each opponent once the regular season begins, and it's easy for a coach to become consumed with this type of specific game preparation, but here's the question: What good does it do to have a great game plan if the players executing it aren't skilled enough in the fundamentals to carry it out and compete?

The answer is obvious—a game plan is worthless without players well versed in the fundamentals. Knowing this, each of our practice sessions begins with a pre-practice period during which the players have a fifteen-minute ritual of working on different fundamentals. These segments—led by my assistants—run from 2:50-3:05 each day. As a staff, we carefully plan the pre-practice sessions to rotate different drills so *all of the fundamentals* are *routinely* covered.

There *are* certain skills that we work on every day, and because the bottom line in any basketball game is putting the ball in the basket, shooting is always involved during the pre-practice ritual. Along with shooting, different drills, sometimes position-specific, will be incorporated into the plan and rotated so that we make sure we are covering all of the fundamental bases on a weekly basis. No matter how advanced the player, he needs daily fundamental work to keep his skills sharp.

The fifteen-minute pre-practice session establishes a definite objective at the outset of each practice, and it gets everyone in the right frame of mind; also, it allows the players to take ownership of their improvement while they develop a work ethic. Once the practice session begins, it is my job to make evaluating the fundamentals of our players an ongoing process so that we can continue to plan pre-practice time to meet *their* needs.

When the pre-practice period ends, I call the team together and give them our thought for the day. I try to make the thought of the day a quick motivating idea that helps get the team focused on the daily practice. Sometimes I pull a quote from a prominent person and other times I have my own thought. Either way, *the thought of the day* has been a good way to get the players centered and ready to listen to me.

Once the body of the practice starts, my plans consist primarily of drills—very little outright scrimmaging. We do some live 5-on-5, but it is done possession by possession—in a controlled environment—with some very specific goals in mind. For example, if we are working on executing our half-court delay game, the offense will start with the ball and we will focus that segment of our practice on all the things required for success in this area: sound fundamentals, good decision-making, floor balance, and understanding of game situations—like score and clock. We want to simulate game situations the best we can and use our practice time to teach the players to understand what we are trying to accomplish at all times. The general objective I keep in mind when making each practice schedule is to build players who are *physically and mentally prepared for every situation*.

As for the specific goals of each practice, the most important aspects of our system are repeated daily and show up in different drills—and the fundamentals of the game keep coming back into play. If one were to observe one of my practices, shooting, passing, screening, dribbling, defensive sliding, pivoting—and *even more* passing would be seen.

The reason for listing passing twice is because I believe passing is the most important aspect of offensive *team* basketball. I want an overwhelming majority of our points to come via the assist, because I think the mark of a well-coached team is that it is a great passing team. This concept promotes teamwork and empowers every player on the floor to be a part of *the plan* on offense. Like the other fundamentals, becoming a good passing team does not happen by accident—it is mastered through constant practice.

In one of our practices, an observer will see passing being practiced in a number of ways, from two-player drills all the way up to our 5-on-5 back door offense. A good passing team is a good offensive team; a great passing team tends to be a great offensive team; and, on the flip side, a bad passing team tends to dribble itself into offensive oblivion. At Triway and at Hoover, our practice plans have always reflected the importance I place on passing as a staple of team basketball.

When I try to summarize my thoughts on planning my daily practices, I go back to a conversation I once had the opportunity to have—face-to-face—with UCLA's legendary coach John Wooden. Coach Wooden once told me: *The game of basketball is merely mastering the fundamentals of the game and being able to execute them quickly at a high level.* I always keep that in mind when I construct my daily practice plans, and I spend countless hours during a season evaluating our players in practice and on film.

I then use what I observe in my players to carefully plan the *next* practice so that my players continue to develop the capability of executing the fundamentals within our system at a high level under the pressure of game speed. It's an ongoing cycle from November through late March to prepare our players to be physically and mentally prepared in every way they can be. As the head coach, *the CEO of a high school basketball corporation*, I feel like one of my most important basketball-related jobs is to carefully plan each practice throughout the course of the season so I put my team in the best position I can to help it experience success.

100 (Kramer)

After I had worked for a couple years as an assistant for Henry Cobb at Canton South High School early in my career, he once said to me, "*Matt, I feel that you like game nights way too much.*" At the time I felt it was one of the strangest things I'd ever heard another coach say to me.

I did love the games! We were winning at the varsity and junior varsity levels; we were playing in front of full houses; and there was action and excitement all the time. I enjoyed practices, too, but of course I liked game nights—they were exhilarating. I had no idea why my mentor would tell me I liked the games too much; I thought he was crazy.

Fifteen years later, I look back and realize how spot on his comment was—because after being a head coach for eleven years—I enjoy practice time far more than I enjoy game night. Why? Because practice is the only place in the game of basketball a coach can *control* the environment to master successful execution. No coach has that power on game night—try as we might. Practice is the only place.

Once a head coach, I quickly learned that—although minor adjustments can certainly have a big impact on the outcome of a particular game—almost 100% of what the audience sees on game night has been firmly established through hours of practice. In other words, fair or not, game night is a chance for the entire world to show up and judge how well a coach is performing his job. Therefore, practice is the place I shape what I want our fans, community and administrators to see. This obviously means that I believe a head coach should place a great deal of importance on daily practice.

Like Coach Montgomery said in his section, preparing a practice plan should be something in which a head coach takes great care in doing every day. As the year goes on, some of the content of *my daily practice plan* will change to meet the game-planning needs for a certain opponent, and I am also a big believer that the amount of time spent on the practice floor needs to be reduced late in the season to keep kids fresh and energized on game nights. However, I try never to allow game planning, reduction in practice time, or any other variable to interfere with my daily practice commitment to the fundamentals of the game *and* our system staples.

The first question I ask myself before I start putting any practice plan together is this: *What do I want us to be good at doing?* Then I create a practice plan that will lead to us being good at those things. For example, I believe in instituting an up-tempo style of play. At Fairless— then at Canton South—the program personnel strengths were in athletic guards who had a certain degree of skill. At Fairless especially, we also had some nice 6'3" to 6'5" kids sprinkled in who fit well into a running game, but we never really had that true big guy that we could pound the ball into for consistent scoring. In a typical half-court game, we struggled getting productivity out of our fours and fives—typically known as "bigs" in today's basketball vernacular—so we picked up the pace to get everyone in a space where each player could function to the best of his ability. At Fairless we became very good at it; at South we were on the verge of being good at it. The difference? Practice.

Just about every segment of my practices has a *running- game* component built in, *because the fast break is a fundamental staple of our system.* For players to believe that I really want them to play at a fast pace I have to teach them the skills to play at that fast pace; to trust in my vision— *my best-laid plans*—I have to make my vision tangible to them by weaving it into the fabric of our daily workouts. Hours of planning go into my daily practice plans throughout the course of a season, and those daily plans are timed to the minute—from the time the players walk on the floor till the very end—to maximize productivity.

Like Coach Montgomery, my players walk onto the floor with a partner and they engage in pre-practice individual fundamental work in shooting, ball-handling and passing every day; After pre-practice, the next 15-20 minutes of live practice mixes in a number of drills we consistently do to master the fundamentals of the running game. Early in the development of a program and, in reality, the first few practices of every season, these drills will make those on the sidelines feel like they are in a dodge-ball game gone awry—the ball will be flying all over the gym. In fact, each season when practice opens I kid the guys that we will need to issue helmets to all of the spectators to protect them when they sit in the stands if we don't get better at passing and catching while playing at a high speed. But we always *do* get better through these drills, because I show the players my commitment to the development of these skills by including them in practice on a daily basis.

I had a local coach ask me after my Fairless team won the *Canton Division-II District Championship* in 2007 how I get my kids to play at such a fast pace. I told him the answer is simple: *we practice it every day— it's really not any more complicated than that.*

From there, the practice moves on to other aspects of play. We break things down defensively, offensively, out-of-bounds situations— everything possible to prepare for every situation—just like any other program. The difference with my system is that we *never* leave the running game. I try to incorporate offensive and defensive transition into every drill we do—from 2-on-2 all the way up to 5-on-5. The way we are attempting to play, there is no use in checking the ball up at half-court after *every* possession, so I like to work on things in *three-possession bursts.*

For instance, if we start with the ball and our focus is on fine-tuning our half-court execution against a man-to-man defense, we will also be working on press defense on a made shot and transition defense on a miss. Once on defense, we play through the stop or score. The third possession in the sequence is what I call "free time"—the first nine seconds of gaining possession of the ball. During this time, the original offensive team—the group that started with the ball—is back on offense, working on attacking the defense in transition on made *and* missed shots. After the third possession—a sequence that goes half-court offense to transition or press defense to "free time"—I stop play and we start another *three-possession burst.* In organizing practice in this manner, we focus on one thing—in this case half-court offense—*but we continue to commit to our running game and creating an up-tempo.*

When we flip the focus to half-court defense, we simply reverse the order of *the three-possession burst*—defense to transition offense to transition defense. First, the ball starts at half-court and we work at getting a stop, much like any team would do when working on its half-court defense. Again, the difference with me is that we are going to run our transition offense whether we get a stop or not. Sometimes *I* force the action in transition by requiring a shot within the first nine seconds of gaining possession; sometimes I tell them to go from "free time" and "flow" into a full offensive possession if we don't get what we're after right away. Either way, I believe a running team *must* be able to develop a mindset that it can run effectively on makes and misses, so I commit to it in practice.

Of course, if it begins to look like the guys have decided that giving up easy baskets is a good way to get the ball back, we alter the drill, but typically this doesn't happen. Kids tend to innately work hard within the framework of the *three-possession concept*, so it's a rare occasion I have to motivate them to play hard. Hey, it's a lot like playing basketball, and that's what they all came out to do, right?

The final component of practice I want to mention is shooting. When I went to observe one of Coach Montgomery's practices at the end of the 2009 season during his Hoover team's run to a district title, I do as I always do when observing a great coach at work. I search for one thing I can take to make my practices better. The thing I took that March day was that his kids came out of the locker room *together* and they came out *with a purpose*. There was none of the idle standing around and unproductive action that can characterize the time kids spend waiting for their coaches to start giving orders. The way Coach Montgomery's practice started didn't leave the kids any choice—it was either get productive or get left behind.

I liked that, so I modified Coach Montgomery's idea to fit the needs of my practices. I decided I wanted the goal of my players—as soon as they hit the floor—to be developing into confident and consistent shooters. So, I came up with the following procedure that would teach them to be self-directed in pursuing the goal:

Every player has a permanent partner and neither member of the tandem can leave the locker room and enter the gym for pre-practice without the other. Once on the floor, each pair will partake in our *lock-in shooting drill* established to form and maintain good shooting habits—and they will work at this until the coaches stop them to give new directions. A diligent pair will get a chance to get between 50-75 shots each before any directions have been given during the first seven to ten minutes they are on the floor.

After the first seven to ten minutes of partner lock-in time, position coaches may take certain groups to a basket and work on specific aspects of the game—like post work or individual ball-handling. But every practice starts with shooting. *I want my players to get more shots up than any other players in the State of Ohio*, and that starts with getting them to step onto the floor with a partner and a purpose. Starting each practice with our *partner lock-in shooting* has been tremendously successful in the capacity of building better shooters, but this tactic actually has a second powerful purpose

It also puts some peer pressure on players to get to practice as quickly as they can. I have found an unhappy player sitting in the locker room constantly waiting for his partner to finish arguing with his girlfriend tends to eventually be a good cure for that problem. Most kids want to shoot, and allowing them to start practice by getting shots is a motivating factor in getting them focused—and getting them there on time.

Our *lock-in shooting routine* has produced some of the most prolific three-point shooters in the history of the State of Ohio, including Stark County's all-time leader in three-point shots made, Jerry Prestier. My players know this, so they have bought into the shooting routine.

Once the pre-practice time has ended, my practice plan continues to make shooting a priority throughout the practice, including another segment at the end of practice that is dedicated to our *"machine-gun shooting drill"*. The goal during the *machine-gun drill* is for each perimeter player to *take* 100 threes in ten minutes. We don't always get there, but we always get close. My philosophy is: *If we're going to use the three-point shot as a weapon, it's my job to create three-point shooters.* I believe that can be done through repetition, just like I believe creating an excellent running game can be done through a commitment to it in practice. Anyone who has ever witnessed one of my teams' practices has come away understanding the commitment I make to both the running game and the three-point shot.

When a program *is* having success, it invariably draws interest from other people in the game to want to watch a practice. I seek to find coaches like Coach Montgomery every year that will allow me to observe and learn from them, and I would encourage every coach, young or experienced, to do the same. The people who have witnessed my teams' practices have always walked away with the lasting impression that we practice with a high energy level and spirit, and our style of play on game nights is reflective of the practice plan. Regardless of what style a coach chooses to install, I think high energy, spirited effort, and practice action that reflects the style of play a team displays on game nights, are all pretty good goals for a coach to have when he sits down to create his daily practice plan.

Today, there's no place I'd rather be than practice, because practice is where I have an opportunity to shape the way my team plays on game nights. When my Fairless teams became great at practice, we became a championship-caliber program—so game nights also continued to be a lot of fun. I suspect that's what Henry Cobb was trying to get me to understand years ago when he told me he thought I liked the games way too much.

9

Discipline:

Making the tough decisions

500

There are a few things that I believe quietly cultivate discipline in a program. Here they are:

1) Be on time to all team functions.

2) Ties are worn to school and on the bus to away games.

3) Shirts are tucked in at practice.

4) Address the officials with respect at all times.

5) Hair is at an acceptable length.

Now that those have been established, allow me to suggest that the list above is the easy part and that real discipline runs far deeper than anything the above list openly displays. *Real discipline* is being able to make the tough decisions—the art of doing what is in the best interest of *teaching* each individual player to become the best person he can possibly become while also keeping in mind the best interest of the program—an art that I feel evolves as a head coach gains experience.

How has my idea of discipline evolved? Simple: *I used to have many rules and few suggestions; today I have few rules and many suggestions.* In my early days as a head coach at Triway High School, I would pass out a three-page list of rules that addressed every situation a coach could think possible—with consequences to match the infractions. This 'older-school' approach was not a bad one by any means. However, because life is continuously changing and new situations are constantly arising, no coach could ever imagine and outline every disciplinary scenario that may present itself. So, I don't even try anymore.

I have found that a much shorter list of *expectations*—not rules—has actually allowed me to be more of a *leader* and *teacher* and less of a traffic cop. Specific rules and consequences are black and white, and when black and white are mixed together they provide gray areas for the *players*. Expectations provide *me—the leader*—with the gray areas that give me the flexibility to do what is in the best interest of educating a young man and act in the best interest of running the basketball program. Here's an example that explains what I mean:

In today's day and age, a player might claim he didn't know he wasn't allowed to bring a cell phone to practice and text when he was on the sideline—because there is no specific rule in the packet I gave him that says that. Hey, I never imagined a player could think bringing a cell phone to practice *would be* ok, so I didn't list "no cell phones at practice" in my rules. I thought common sense would tell a basketball player he shouldn't have his cell phone in the gym during practice.

As ridiculous as this scenario sounds, the fact is, my long list of rules did *not* contain a policy on texting during practice, so logically and legally the player *could* challenge any consequence I passed down for what, to me, was an obvious—albeit unstated—infraction.

To avoid having to defend disciplining nonsense that is not listed as a specific rule—such as a player texting during practice—I write an expectation that allows me to be a *leader*:

"During the 2-3 hours our players spend on the practice floor they are expected to put full focus, commitment, and dedication into basketball and basketball only."

Now, I doubt any player would ever bring a cell phone to practice and text, but that expectation gives players zero wiggle room to screw around, tell jokes, daydream, or anything else that might take away from getting the most out of a practice. The expectation is short, concise, and it teaches a player what he should be doing; it does not list what he shouldn't be doing. It's a lead-management approach to setting rules and it has an impact that goes beyond the 'cat and mouse' game that can accompany a scroll of specific rules. I believe this form of discipline not only is the best way to instill lasting results in my players, but it also allows me to forge solid relationships with my players as their mentor.

The impact a coach has on the young people he or she mentors is lasting; it would be impossible for a coach just starting out to understand the significance of his effect on players over the long haul. But as

I've grown older—as players have come back and thanked me for the influence I have had on them—it has become more tangible to me. The impression a head coach makes on a young person is a *powerful* thing.

Knowing this, I always get a feel for the team and its players, and deal with discipline accordingly—meaning that I feel it is my responsibility to make disciplinary decisions that are fair both to the player and to the team. Allow me to share a couple of examples:

During the 2009 tournament season, we earned the right to play in the District Championship Game against Canton Timken. Because the winner would earn a berth into the Regional Tournament and the State of Ohio's *Division-I "Sweet-16"*, it was easily the biggest game of our season—and maybe the biggest of my tenure at North Canton Hoover. The morning of that game, a Saturday in the middle of March—I scheduled a walk-through and shoot-around, just as I would on the morning of any Saturday game. Problem was, our starting center—Tyler Fausnight—was significantly late because he overslept and missed his ride.

Therefore, I had to find a consequence for Tyler without disrupting the mission—while also maintaining the accountability I had put in place for *all* players. This was a very delicate undertaking, so I carefully considered all the variables and did what I felt was best for Tyler, his teammates, and the program.

Taking into consideration that he had been a shining example of the type of person we want our program to stand for, I knew it would be unfair to Tyler to pass down a punishment so harsh as suspending him for the entire game—the consequence for missing a practice outlined in my old three-page set of rules. Moreover, knowing that the team was very tight-knit and unified made me realize it would also be unfair to Tyler's teammates to punish him too harshly, because it would compromise their collective goal that they had set out to achieve since day one of practice in November—winning a District Championship.

With the help of my staff, I came to the conclusion that the appropriate consequence for Tyler was to be kept out of the first quarter of play that night. In doing this, my staff and I felt we were being fair to the team as a whole without breaking from our philosophy of teaching our players that it is important to be accountable for their actions.

Not always—but I have found that in many cases—when a coach makes the tough decision and does the right thing, the team responds and plays well enough to be victorious. As it turned out, we did hold

Tyler out of the first quarter of action that Saturday night, and the team used that as a rallying point to play one of the most inspired games I've ever coached in upsetting Canton Timken—the team widely believed to be destined for a berth in the *Final Four*. It was a huge victory for Hoover—but perhaps a bigger victory for the power of discipline.

In this next situation, the variables called for a bit heavier hand. Early in my career at Triway, I had a tremendously talented and athletic sophomore post player. Even though he was only in tenth grade, he was a star, and he knew it—to the point that he thought he was above the rules that the rest of the team had to follow. A situation arose with this young man prior to the first game that season over—of all things—the team shoes I chose for our players.

That year, the 1985-86 season, I decided that all of our players would wear the same shoes—*purple Chuck Taylor's*. Allow me to go on record right now as saying that nobody particularly liked my choice—including my wife. The shoes were a five-star fashion *faux pas*, but I didn't care.

After practice the night before the opening game, one of my captains—a hard-working team player by the name of Doran Braun—came to me and said that 'our star player' told everyone in the locker room that he *would not* wear the shoes. I knew he was a huge key to a great season, but I told Doran that the talented sophomore wouldn't be playing in that first game—or any other game—until he purchased and agreed to wear the team shoes.

Now, I'm a big believer that a coach has to pick his battles, and—in retrospect—allowing the players to have a say in their team shoes, as I do today, would have been a way to avoid this conflict. But the situation with this young man wasn't really about some ugly purple shoes, and it was far different from the one I would confront with Tyler Fausnight some twenty-five years later at Hoover. In Tyler's situation, he was a senior with a long history of great character playing for a very unified, *established* team in a successful program; he made the mistake of oversleeping and felt badly about it. In the situation with the young star at Triway, he was a tenth grader who had *never* played a varsity basketball game, on a team and program that was still trying to establish a successful identity—and he was *choosing* not to follow a very basic team rule. If it hadn't been the shoes with this young man, it would have been something else down the line. I'm a big believer that the sooner a problem is headed off, the better.

I also knew the whole program was watching to see how I would deal with this issue; I knew that not playing him that night because he refused to wear the purple shoes might very well cost us an early season game. But, I also knew that allowing him to do his own thing and play in that game, win or lose, would have been far more harmful to the long-term good of the program than losing one basketball game. Simply put, I decided he would not play unless he wore the shoes.

I looked at the situation as an opportunity to teach—not just my prize sophomore—the entire program. The message a coach must send early in establishing a program is simple: Hey, he may be our best player, guys, but if he isn't going to have the discipline to follow the rules, he isn't going to play at Triway.

I really think this young man went home the night before that first game thinking that there was no way I would hold him out of a game over a pair of shoes. However, when he showed up to the gym the next night for the game and I had not moved off of my stance, he finally *did* realize I was very serious about him either getting the shoes or sitting out. Somewhat in shock, he came to me right before the junior varsity game started and told me he wanted the shoes.

Well, getting purple Chuck Taylor's in a size 15 wasn't easy at any time, much less a couple hours from tip-off on a Friday night, so I thought he was probably out of luck. But, I had my assistant make a call to the local sporting goods store to see what they could do for us. As luck would have it for this young man, the store had one pair of white *Chuck Taylor's* in a size 15, so he took the white canvas shoes and silk-screened purple on them for us, and rushed them over to the gym shortly before we went on the floor for warm-ups.

The team played great that night when star sophomore Larry Benning put those hideous purple shoes on and took his first steps toward being a two-time All-Ohio. However, the most important thing that night was that I held my ground with the entire program watching me, and sent a message that was a major victory for me in building Triway into a program that would enjoy a strong tradition of success, including making two trips to the State of Ohio's *Final Four* in Columbus—one of those in 1988, Larry Benning's senior season.

I chose to share the disciplinary situations with Larry Benning at Triway in 1985 and Tyler Fausnight at Hoover in 2009, as they were two of the biggest decisions as a leader that I've ever had to make, and because they were situations with contrasting variables. Tyler was a player with a long track record of being an upstanding member of a successful program who made a mistake by oversleeping; Larry was a sophomore with tremendous talent who felt his talent made him above the rules. Tyler made his mistake the day of the big game; Larry made his mistake when the "big game" was but a dream somewhere on the horizon for a program building an identity. Had I handled either of those situations wrong, it would have compromised the long-term prospects for success of both the Triway and Hoover programs. In the end, the fact is this: Both programs became championship programs with those two players playing major roles because of the careful consideration put into selecting the proper form of discipline for the players—discipline that kept the best interests of the player and his teammates in mind.

Ultimately, discipline is not about purple shoes or malfunctioning alarm clocks; discipline is about love, and love isn't about saying yes to everything. Love is doing what is best for the person—even when it hurts. It is tough love, but it's love nonetheless. I loved my program at Triway and the players in that program just as I love my program at North Canton Hoover and the players I have coached and currently coach. In my opinion, there isn't enough real love in the world today.

Many parents mistake love for sheltering their child. It's just the opposite. Young people learn most when they fail and are corrected. Beyond winning basketball games, I thoroughly enjoy having the opportunity to impact the lives of my players and help them develop into self-disciplined, responsible, and persevering members of society. Don't think a coach has that much influence? Then consider this:

Rick Rottman and Stan "Coke" Starr, two men who had sons who were terrific players for me, once told me when I was at Triway that I had a greater impact on their sons than they did. I had never really thought of that, so I didn't necessarily believe them. Seeing that I was skeptical, they began to explain that I had their sons for over two hours every day—in a captive setting that the kids enjoyed. Mr. Rottman and Mr. Star proceeded to tell me that they *never* had the opportunity to spend two uninterrupted, captive hours in a row with their sons; daily life just doesn't offer such windows of time. That really hit home with me—as it should with every coach or leader of young people.

100 (Kramer)

In his book titled *Wins, Losses and Lessons*, Lou Holtz wrote, "Discipline is not what you do to someone, but rather what you do for someone." In all of the reading and studying I've done of other coaches in every sport, I've never found a quote that more captures the essence of the way discipline ought to be viewed by a high school basketball coach.

My experiences have led me to believe that being a public school head basketball coach allows me to make a deep-rooted positive impact on a young person, and that is a responsibility I take very seriously—far more seriously than I take winning a basketball game.

I have been a head coach in two very fine communities—Fairless High School, a mid-sized, rural, blue-collar community; and Canton South High School, a mid-sized, blue-collar town that uniquely melds some farmland with some inner city. So whereas I am not an expert on being a head coach in an inner city setting, I do have experience working with a very diverse group of young men. Here's the point: Every player is going to bring certain things to the table according to his life experiences, and some kids have simply had things more difficult growing up than others. It is my job to help them all—in every way possible. However, here is one of the theories that I have developed in my time as a head coach to which I hold firmly: I will never allow *helping* a player to turn into *enabling* a player.

After being in coaching for over twenty years, more than a decade of that as a head coach—I have come to find that a coach's ability to make the tough disciplinary decisions is probably the biggest factor in dictating the long-term success of his program. Like Coach Montgomery, I used to pass out a multiple-page player code of conduct with all kinds of rules and consequences outlined in writing; also like Coach Montgomery, I no longer do that, because I finally listened to my own advice.

One of my favorite things to tell my players when things get moving too fast in a game is to *find simplicity where there seems to be chaos.* Handing players a packet with a bunch of rules and consequences can cause chaos, so I simplified by boiling everything down into one simple expectation and put it on a paper that I require both my players and their parents to sign before the season starts. The expectation reads as follows:

Any player who does anything that could be detrimental to the team—on or off the court—will be subject to disciplinary action deemed appropriate by Coach Kramer and his staff.

In my early years as a head coach, I quickly discovered a long black and white list of rules *enabled* players to find ways into gray areas, and in those cases, the specific rules actually limited my ability to lead and do what would be best for the players and the program. I truly believe that the way my one *expectation* reads gives me the flexibility I need to be an effective leader and a positive contributor to helping my players build the self-discipline they need to be successful in life. Allow me to share the three trickiest examples of disciplinary decisions I have confronted—the ones that I believe have shaped my current philosophy of discipline.

Example One: The New Year's Eve Party

In my second year as a head coach, I had a tremendous team at Fairless and we were off to a 9-1 start. It was just after the New Year in 2002, and things were rolling. There was a great chemistry to go along with plenty of skill, and it looked like the sky was going to be the limit for that team. No sooner than we had wrapped up a particularly big double-overtime victory over league foe Tusky Valley High School—a victory that put us in sole possession of first place in the conference and avenged the one loss we had suffered early in the season—word came to me through my building principal that several of my players were under police investigation for their participation in underage drinking and some other "things" that had happened at a New Year's Eve party. The six weeks following may have been the most difficult of my coaching career.

When my principal first gave me the news of the party, I didn't even stop to ask who the players were—I was ready to dismiss them immediately.

At that point my principal told me two things: first, he cautioned me to be careful, because they were players who were key to the success of the team, and it was uncertain as to what, if anything, they had done at the party; second, he told me that he had already looked over the code of conduct I had passed out at the beginning of the season and the rules that governed the entire athletic department, and no rule stated I had the power to remove a player who was under an investigation for a *possible* infraction.

This conversation initially angered me, but he told me that I had no legal right to remove a player who had not been found guilty of anything. *My* argument was that they should have cared enough about the program and their teammates to avoid putting themselves in that position. My principal did not disagree, but litigation being what it is nowadays, he also told me that the sensitive nature of the situation was one that was going to have to be handled to the letter of the rules outlined in the paperwork the students were asked to sign prior to the season. In other words, the players were in a gray area, and there was nothing for me to do but let it play out.

So for two weeks it played out. Every day it was something. Scores of kids—including five of my basketball players—were pulled in and out of classes and practices as new evidence was uncovered about the activities at that party—each kid doing his or her best cover-up job so as not to get the others in trouble. Call it 'Partygate' or whatever fits— one thing was for sure—it was a distraction of the worst possible kind and it shed a real renegade light on our program. The kids who had gone to the party were not bad kids; in fact, a couple of them, going out on a limb, I would call great kids. But they made a really poor choice and in doing so compromised the success of the season and destroyed the reputation of the program for a period of time.

Worse, because of my elaborate list of rules—a list that allowed me to do nothing until due process took its course—the situation made me look like I was sheltering my players from the consequences that come with poor choices for the sake of winning some basketball games. Like I said, the moment I was informed of the investigation through the end of that season was perhaps the most difficult six weeks of my coaching career—when it should have been a time of great enjoyment.

The 2001-02 season ended with Fairless winning the conference championship, our fine All-Ohio guard Jerry Prestier being named Conference Player of the Year, and our team finishing with 17 wins. Regardless of the mistakes some of them made in showing up at a party that must have rivaled scenes from the 1980's box-office comedy *Weird Science*, I truly love the players from that team—several still stay in contact with me on almost a daily basis. But the mistakes those five players made forced me to rethink the manner in which I wanted to be able to discipline—leading me to the one expectation that I require every player and their parents to acknowledge and sign before we step on the practice floor the first day. Here it is again:

Any player who does anything that could be detrimental to the team—on or off the court—will be subject to disciplinary action deemed appropriate by Coach Kramer and his staff.

How would having this *expectation* instead of the long list of rules have changed my handling of the New Year's Eve party of 2002? Simple: I would have had the opportunity to be a leader and choose the course of action that would have been best for my program. Specifically, I would have suspended every player involved until the investigation had been completed. That may sound harsh, but it would have been the right thing to do.

As it played out, one of the five basketball players stepped forward and took responsibility for some things that went on at that party, and athletic department rules suspended him for four games. The worst part was that the other four basketball players were likely to have done the same things at the party, but because there was no way to prove it, they continued to play. It was dirty in every way it could be, and I felt like I had failed—albeit with the best intentions in mind—to be the type of *leader* my program needed. It was a program setback and a career setback, and I was determined to never let it happen again.

Now, the expectation itself is very solid, but it's even more effective after I explain it a bit at the annual meeting I have with the players and their parents prior to the start of our practices in the fall. When I pass the form out which states that one expectation, I also include some examples in my presentation—and I always start with a hypothetical New Year's Eve party that my players should not attend. Everyone knows going into the season that if a player is at such a party and is under investigation for wrongdoing, that player will be suspended from all basketball activities until the investigation is complete. I explain that one of the things successful people do is make good choices and placing one's self at such a party during basketball season is simply a poor choice that would carry severe consequences. I tell them that my experience has led me to believe that the distractions caused by allowing a player to continue to participate while being investigated for wrongdoing at such a party would be unfair to every other player and coach, and it would shed a negative light on our basketball family. I have found that—because parents typically don't want their kids at that party either—the adults in the room are in agreement with my expectation and my example.

Like Coach Montgomery said in his section, discipline is love, but it's tough love. Having to make the tough decision is not the fun part of the job, but it is the part that allows a coach to really positively impact his players and prepare them for the world in which they will need to make a living. I don't care how much the world changes, people who exhibit discipline tend to be the ones who have the most success; therefore, self-discipline is perhaps the best quality a coach can instill in his players.

Also like Coach Montgomery suggested, variables will dictate how heavy a hand a coach needs to use to make disciplinary decisions. By the time I left Fairless, I had been there eight years and the players in my program knew what I expected and were highly unlikely to test the boundaries. They knew I was going to rule harshly if they attended that New Year's Eve party; they knew that I expected them to stay out of detention and in-school suspensions; they knew I expected their attendance at school and practice to be impeccable; they knew I held the time we spent on the practice floor sacred. There were very few issues the last four or five years I spent at Fairless. However, when a problem did arise—as difficult as it sometimes was when dealing with young men I truly loved as members of my basketball family—I was always willing to make the tough decision. And it always paid off for the program and the player—always.

Example 2: Taming a Fiery Star.

From the 2004-05 through the 2007-08 seasons I coached a freakishly skilled 5'8" guard named Jordan Jennings. (He was actually closer to 5'5" when he first played varsity as a ninth grader.) Jordan had skill to spare—amazing range; great ball-handling ability; and he was perhaps the best passer I've ever coached—and he was a fiery competitor. The problem Jordan had was his 'fire' was sometimes put on display and channeled in the wrong direction, for example at referees. Now, far be it from me to claim that showing frustration toward an official is not understandable, but I am of the belief that it really cannot be tolerated when a player is doing it.

In 2006-07, Jordan was having a terrific junior year. He was a 5'8" left-handed scoring machine who was literally worth the price of admission. His range started as soon as he crossed half court; his fearless drives to the basket—over, around and through bigger defenders—

116

were remarkable; and his vision and passing brought people out of their seats. After fifteen games, he was averaging over 20 points and 7 assists, and the team was reaping the benefits of the rebuilding process that had been going on since Jordan's freshman year by having solid success against some very good opponents. Problem was, the more success Jordan had, the more he chirped openly in the direction of officials and at opposing players.

As the season wore on, some of the chatter was met with a warning, and in one instance it was met with a technical foul. In the case of a first technical foul, my stance has always been to pull the player out of the game for what I deem an appropriate amount of time for him to cool off and make him understand that such things would not be tolerated. (The standard consequence for a player's second career technical, in the absence of extenuating circumstances, has been removal from the remainder of that game, regardless of how much time is left on the clock.) Jordan never picked up a second technical foul his junior year, but he did have a meltdown that I felt was at least as bad, if not worse.

Late in the 2006-07 season, we hosted league rival and two-time defending *Ohio D-II Runners-up*, Wooster Triway, in front of a standing-room-only crowd. Triway was an amazing program built from ground zero by Randy Montgomery and maintained to a level of excellence by new head coach Keith Snoddy, who took over when Coach Montgomery left for Hoover. Triway had been bullying us with great teams since joining our conference two years earlier as we rebuilt, and going into the season we felt that 2006-07 would be the year we would get over the Triway hump.

In our first meeting with Triway that season we lost a classic double-overtime contest in front of a standing-room-only crowd in "The Pit"—the legendary Triway gym where the purple and white Triway Titans hadn't lost a game in over two years. Following that game—feeling as though we let one get away—we circled '*Round 2*' at our place on the calendar as the night we would slay the Titans.

The second game was another classic battle between two teams that seemed to have a healthy competitive disliking for each other—with the conference championship on the line. The score went back and forth most of the game and delighted the crowd, as no team ever held more than a six-point advantage. As the clock ticked below two minutes, Triway held a one-point lead when a two-possession sequence—defined by two whistles—swung the game in Triway's favor.

I think it's important to point out here that both whistles could have gone either way; they were fifty-fifty calls that make me glad I'm not a referee. At our end, our post player, Josh Brinley, caught the ball at the elbow, drove to his right and scored as there was heavy contact with a Triway defender. I've watched the play on film, and I honestly don't know if it was a block or a charge. Had it been a block, the basket would have been good, and we would have led by one and had a free throw coming. But it was called a charge—no basket; Triway ball with a one-point lead.

At the other end of the floor—on the very next play—our outstanding defensive guard, Stan Soehnlen, stepped in the path of a driving Triway player and drew heavy contact as the ball was laid in the basket. Watching it over and over, again, I can honestly say it could have gone either way—block or charge. Again, at times officials have an impossible job, because someone is always going to be unhappy on those fifty-fifty calls, and this time the call was a block on our defender. The basket counted and the free throw was made; we trailed by four with thirty seconds to play, and we weren't handling it well as a group, especially Jordan.

At this point, I think it's important to acknowledge that I have left out the names of players in some cases because the names were not important to the moral of the story. In this case, I *am* using Jordan Jennings' name because *who* he was goes to the heart of the story. Jordan cared so incredibly much about Fairless Basketball because he had poured every fiber of his being into the rebuilding process that was aimed at being able to beat state power Triway. I will go on record as saying that I have *never* loved a player more than I love Jordan Jennings for the passion he brought to the program each and every day he was with me for four years. But it was my job to teach him how to better channel his passion.

After the two whistles went against us, I called a timeout—after all, we were only down four points, there was still over a minute to go in the game, and we still had two more timeouts. With our firepower, the game was not necessarily decided if we could keep our composure and continue to execute. But we were not able to do either, and that's why we lost the game—a lesson that would pay huge dividends when we met the Triway Titans for a third time in the District Championship game about a month later.

After stressing to the players in the locker room that we lost the game because we didn't handle adversity very well down the stretch, and that Triway had handled it like the champion it was, I was ready to move on and start focusing on the tournament drawing that would be held that Sunday. I knew the players were disheartened, because that night had been our chance to stake claim to a share of a league title two years after the same players—in their youth—began the 2004-2005 season 0-12. It was our focus for two years, we had come within inches of getting it done, and now we were all dealing with the fact that we had fallen painfully short. I knew the next steps by me as a leader were going to be crucial in regaining a focus on creating the special memories that were still attainable, and I knew it wouldn't be easy.

When I left the locker room and went upstairs to meet my family, the mood was understandably somber. Heck, everyone knew how much that night meant to our players and community and, whereas the team had done itself proud with its effort, the fact remained that losing was disappointing. After talking with my friends and family for a few minutes, my top assistant and close friend, Tim Vick, approached me and asked me if I had seen what JJ (Jordan Jennings) did after the final buzzer had sounded. I told him I had not seen anything, and asked what he did. Tim then told me he had not seen it either, but word spread that Jordan had gotten up into the face of an official as the official was trying to leave the floor and verbally *blasted* him.

I didn't want to believe it. I had spoken repeatedly to Jordan about being careful with the way he spoke to officials and I was positive that he understood my message. I thought to myself that I'd talk to Jordan about it, but that I wasn't going to go out of my way to take disciplinary action against him on secondhand information. My job of refocusing the team after falling out of the league race was going to be tough enough; I didn't need any side issues to distract my best player.

Unfortunately for Jordan, our video girl did not turn the camera off quickly enough following the final buzzer, and the next day when I sat down to evaluate the film I saw exactly what was rumored to have happened. In plain view on camera, Jordan Jennings could be seen racing over toward an official immediately following the final buzzer. Once he was in the official's face, he was waving his hands wildly and screaming at him. Of course the camera was too far away to pick up the words, but it didn't matter. Jordan's conduct was clearly unacceptable and detrimental to the team and the image of the program. My job of regrouping and moving forward had just gotten a whole lot tougher.

After showing the film to the rest of my staff, I told them that I felt Jordan had to be suspended for a game even though what he did went unpunished within the rules of the game. I told my staff that I cared about Jordan too much to allow him to think that the fact he was an incredibly gifted basketball player gave him the right to act out in any manner he wanted when he was confronted with disappointment. I felt that simply not starting Jordan or holding him out for a portion of a game was going to send a message to him and the team that I was going to demand the type of discipline and self-control needed for success in life—as long as doing so wouldn't get in the way of us winning a basketball game. That was not the message I wanted to send, so I knew it would be in the best interest of Jordan Jennings and the entire program to suspend him for one game for conduct detrimental to the team.

After the several minor infractions he had committed along the same line, the minor consequences he had incurred had not gotten the job done, and the level of Jordan's insubordination escalated into something that had publicly shed an ugly light on our program and on Jordan. I made my decision to suspend Jordan for one full game because I knew he was a special young man whose potential in this world was unlimited, and I knew he would never reach that potential in basketball or in any aspect of his life until he learned to handle disappointment and respect authority—even when feeling slighted. Of course, just because I was certain I had made the right decision wasn't going to make it any easier to pass on the news to Jordan, who—because of the weekend—two days later still had no idea there was a problem.

Right before our next practice, I called JJ into my office and asked him to sit down. I asked him how he was doing, because I knew he took the loss hard and it was obvious by the look on his face he was still feeling the pain. I wanted Jordan to know I cared about him before I went into the issue. I did not want to ambush him or back him into a corner; actually, I wanted him to see that he had really left me with no choice and that deciding to suspend him, although correct, was agonizing for me as well as him.

After he told me how he was feeling, I asked him if he remembered anything about a conversation he had with an official immediately following the game. At first he wasn't sure what I meant, so I asked him if he approached an official on the floor immediately following the game to voice his displeasure over some calls that didn't go our way. At that point, he kind of hung his head a little bit before looking me in the eyes and acknowledging that he thought he *did* do something to that effect. Once he acknowledged the confrontation, I asked him how bad he thought it looked to those who saw it. He responded by telling me he really didn't remember—which is very believable because of the heat of the moment—but he didn't think it had been *that* bad.

After I allowed him to express himself, I asked him to look at the flat-screen in the office, and I pressed play. I only had to let him see the video once. When I pressed the stop button, he hung his head for a second before looking me in the eyes again, and his exact words were, "That was pretty bad."

I agreed with his assessment and told him that I had already decided to suspend him for the next game, a non-conference game against Marlington. He squirmed a little when I told him, but he also agreed it was fair. He clearly had acted in a manner detrimental to the team, and if I wasn't willing to pass on some meaningful consequences to my best player, there was no reason to have any expectations for anyone. I made sure Jordan knew I cared about him and that it sickened me to have to sit him down. I wanted him to know that I hurt with him.

There were many variables that went into the decision I made to suspend Jordan Jennings, but the most important variable was that I cared about *Jordan Jennings*. Disciplining is caring, because allowing a person to continue to do things that are self-destructive is clearly *not* caring. Had I turned a blind eye to what I saw on that film, I would have been enabling Jordan and setting him up for future failure. Jordan Jennings was a great basketball player and a terrific young man before the incident; however, I believe he became a better basketball player and a better person through this experience.

As it played out, on a snowy Ohio winter night that kept everyone away from the Fairless gym except family and our most staunch supporters, we gave a sluggish performance and lost by one point to a pretty good team from Marlington High School as Jordan served his one-game suspension. Of course I did not want to lose, but I also believed the message I was trying to send those in my program may have been stronger in losing than it would have been in winning. The message was simple: *As the leader of the program, I was not willing to sacrifice discipline and the positive image of our program for the sake of winning a basketball game.*

As a team, we struggled through the loss to Triway and the disciplinary issue with Jordan for a week or so, but all of the adversity and the positive way in which Jordan bounced back strengthened the team and refocused the players for what would be an amazing tournament run.

Jordan finished the 2006-07 season by winning the first of two straight Conference Player of the Year awards; he was selected to the

All-Ohio 3rd team; and, to go along with his other numerous individual honors, he led the 2006-07 Fairless team to *The Canton Division-II District Championship* and a spot in the school's third-ever *"Sweet- 16."* All told, Jordan Jennings finished his career as Fairless' second all-time leading scorer with over 1,200 career points; he broke the school's long-standing single-game scoring record by scoring 54 points against Canton Timken in January of 2008; he broke the school's all-time single-game assist record that same year with 17 against Tuscarawas Valley High School; he won two straight *PAC-7 Conference Player of the Year Awards*; he was named to two straight *All-Ohio* teams; and he was a major factor in leading our program at Fairless out of the darkness and into prominence on a state level.

After graduating, Jordan accepted a scholarship from *Ashland University* to play at the *NCAA D-II* level, and he is currently working toward a degree that may very well lead to a teaching and coaching career. Today Jordan and I remain very close. He has done some volunteer coaching for me in his spare time; we play golf; we go out to dinner; and we talk to each other like old friends do. When he graduates from college, I hope to help Jordan get his career in teaching and coaching started by hiring him onto my staff.

All of that said, I truly believe that our relationship is what it is today because of the respect we have for each other that was built through me disciplining him and him accepting my discipline. I truly believe that there is no relationship that could have a stronger foundation than the ones a coach builds with his players who truly 'get it'. Does this mean every player I have ever coached has liked me and appreciated the things I tried to do for them? Absolutely not. But there is a long list of players with whom I stay in contact, like Jordan Jennings—young men who have thanked me in many ways for the discipline I tried to instill in them.

Example 3: The "Top Dog" Misses Practice.

Jerald Robinson called me from his dorm room at the University of Michigan in April of 2009 to ask me if he could interview me for a paper he was doing for his leadership class. Jerald played for me only one season before accepting a football scholarship to play for the Michigan Wolverines, so I was interested to know why he had chosen me—not one of his football coaches from high school—as the subject of his paper. His response and this story goes to the heart of Coach Holtz's quote I used earlier: Discipline is not what you do *to* somebody; it's what you do *for* somebody. Allow me to share:

The two major reasons I found the Canton South job appealing enough to leave the program I had built at Fairless were that I knew from my time at the school as a young assistant, Canton South was a basketball school in a basketball community, and I also knew that I'd have the opportunity to coach big-time athletes like Jerald Robinson.

When I left Canton South to take the head coaching job at Fairless in 2000, the basketball program at South was as good as it gets. Henry Cobb was a fantastic coach and mentor to me, and he had that program humming. Young boys in Canton Township grew up wanting to be Wildcat varsity basketball players and when they became varsity players, nothing was more important to them than being a part of the basketball program.

When I returned to Canton South in the spring of 2008, I was shocked to find out that basketball was no more than a casual hobby for the players in my new program. I had just left a program at Fairless with highly committed players and expected to see the same when I returned to South. Instead, it was come and go as you please. The program at Canton South was struggling when I took over as head coach because of the lack of importance placed on basketball by the players—a problem I picked up on when I began to run my summer program right after accepting the job in late May.

If I scheduled a workout in our gym, there would be only seven or eight players in attendance; if we had a summer league game at the local recreation center, twenty-five guys would show up. The message from my players to me was pretty simple: *We like to play basketball, but being good at it isn't all that important.* It was really pretty frightening.

I have no idea how this transformation took place—my predecessor, Henry Cobb, was a great coach and respected disciplinarian—but I knew that instilling some discipline back into the program was the only way to make the program relevant to the players again.

I firmly believe that a coach's first big disciplinary decision is crucial to the long-term success of the program, especially when the issue goes to the heart of the program's struggles and, sure enough, my big chance to set the tone for my new program at Canton South for years to follow came the weekend before our first game. The day after Thanksgiving we traveled to Cleveland to scrimmage *Benedictine High School* in their "Meet the

Teams Night" event. I was familiar with Benedictine's team because it had knocked my Fairless team out of the regional tournament two years prior, and I knew it would be a good chance for the players in my new program to see how far they had to go to get where we wanted to be. Sure enough, led by Cameron Wright, a recruit to the *University of Pittsburgh*, Benedictine beat us soundly that Friday night. I felt it was a good lesson for my guys in what it would take to compete at the highest level.

After the long bus ride from Cleveland back to Canton, we arrived at the high school around midnight and I told the players that we would have a light practice and walk-through the next morning at 10:00 a.m. to begin preparing for *Canton Central Catholic*, our opening night opponent the following Friday. I knew that it would be asking too much for a full-scale workout the next morning in light of the scrimmage and late night, so I stressed that the morning would be as much mental preparation as physical.

The next morning I greeted the players in the locker room with donuts and juice. The mood was upbeat despite the beating Benedictine had put on us, because I had stressed to the players the night before that I believed we would beat a team like Benedictine by the end of the season. I also reminded my guys that they had enjoyed good success in all of their other scrimmages and we wouldn't be playing a team like Benedictine any time soon. I wanted their focus to be on the process of developing as a team and creating the type of program that could realistically compete with *the Benedictine's and St. Vincent-St. Mary's* of the world. I felt like the spirit in the locker room was that of a group ready to start taking steps toward excellence. One problem: About halfway through our team stretching, I realized Jerald Robinson wasn't there.

As I've already mentioned, Jerald was the school's top athlete. He had been a starter on the basketball team since he walked into the building as a freshman; he was being recruited by Ohio State and Michigan for football; and he was a player we truly needed if we were to have a chance at being any good at all. In short, Jerald was not a kid we could afford to lose if we were going to win our first game, and everyone knew it.

For the sake of getting the season off to a good start, I sincerely hoped that Jerald was just running a little late. That would give me a chance to pass down some consequences and refocus on the task of beating Central Catholic. As five minutes turned into fifteen, I quietly wished Jerald wouldn't show up at all—I realized that instilling a greater sense of importance on the program in the players would be far more valuable than starting with a victory.

As it turned out, I got my wish. Jerald never came to the gym that morning, and it wasn't until about 5:00 p.m. that Jerald finally did call my cell phone to explain. He told me that he had overslept because his alarm clock didn't go off, and he made sure to let me know that he was sincerely sorry. I told him I understood—sometimes alarm clocks malfunction. I told him he was forgiven and that I looked forward to getting him back to practice to start getting him ready—for the Coventry game a week from Tuesday. He said, "But Coach K, we play Central Catholic *this Friday.*"

I responded, "No Jerald, your teammates play Central Catholic on Friday; missing a practice means you miss a game. Your first game will be game two against Coventry."

There was silence for a minute, then Jerald told me that he thought the morning was just *a light workout and walk through,* and he expressed confusion in understanding why missing something so *short* and *light* should cost him a whole game.

In attempting to make his case, Jerald also defined the program's problems. Jerald Robinson—the top athlete in the school and one of the best athletes in the state—had deemed a light practice in preparation for a game to be unimportant. If the "top dog" deems it unimportant, what importance should the rest of the team place on it? I would say not too much—until I showed them all how important that "light practice" and "walk-through" was *to me.*

When Jerald was done stating his case, I repeated his consequences to him and told him the decision was final. He actually accepted his fate relatively quickly and was never at any point indignant. When I realized he was taking it in stride, I asked him how he had *expected* me to handle his absence. He told me that the rules the year before stated that missing practice for the first time meant a starter would be held out of the starting lineup—Jerald more than likely woke up Saturday morning tired and sore from the night before and just felt like he could live with not starting, so he went back to sleep.

I explained to Jerald that I liked him and thought he could be a really good player for me, but that I also had no interest in coaching players who missed practice. In fact, I told him I'd rather lose games than go through a season wondering who would show up to practice and who wouldn't. This was the first time of several over my first two years at Canton South that I would have an opportunity to prove I meant what I said.

Moving forward, Jerald proved he was a great kid by respectfully accepting his suspension. He showed up to practice all week and got most of his reps with the second group. The night of the Central game, he dressed in a suit and rooted for his teammates as if his life depended on their success. We led most of the game that night, but we ran out of gas and lost in the closing moments. More importantly than anything that could have happened in that game, Jerald Robinson never missed another practice, nor did any of his teammates the rest of that season. The seeds had been sown and the message was clear: *It is important to come to all scheduled team functions; not doing so means not playing in games; and the rules apply to Jerald, so they must apply to everyone.*

After getting off to a slow start, Jerald went on to have a very solid junior year. He averaged over twenty points and ten rebounds a game over the last eleven games of the season, and we forged a very solid relationship. A coach never knows how an athlete of supreme physical ability is going to handle discipline, but that early issue strengthened my relationship with Jerald. My hunch then was that I was the first coach to show him I was willing to lose a game to show him some consequences that mattered to him, and my guess is that he respected that.

My hunch was confirmed a year and a half later when Jerald called me from Michigan after a spring football practice for that phone interview. I told him I was honored that he had chosen me as his most influential coach, then I asked him, "Why me?"

He said, "Coach K, you are the first coach who ever made me work harder than I wanted to work and take things seriously. I never understood what it meant to be a leader until I played for you."

Despite opting for early graduation upon the request of Michigan head football coach Rich Rodriguez—a decision that forced him to forgo his senior season of basketball at Canton South—it pleases me that Jerald Robinson has remained in close contact with me. He is a symbol for all kids who really 'get it'—they want discipline in their lives and they are far more likely to forge strong relationships with leaders who give it to them than they are to forge strong relationships with those who enable them to do as they please. A fact that should make a leader feel like he is doing the right thing *for the young person* when making the tough disciplinary decision.

I chose the examples with Jerald Robinson, Jordan Jennings and the New Year's Eve Party of 2002 because they show a variety of situations and a range of issues that encompass both on-court and off-court problems. In sharing these stories about discipline, I wanted to get two important points across:

126

First, discipline is an issue of leadership and the more flexibility a coach has to make disciplinary decisions, the better leader he will be for his program and the players in it. Second, a coach cannot allow fear of losing a game to figure into the discipline he passes down to a player. I believe if a coach holds true to these two basic concepts, eventually he will have a program disciplined enough to be consistently successful.

10
Constructing a Productive Summer Plan:
From Cincinnati to Chapel Hill;
Bob Huggins & The Wizard of Westwood

500

SUMMER BASKETBALL TODAY is far different than when I played in high school in the 1970's. Back then, there was nothing organized for basketball players to do to get better. Today—in basketball terms—*summer* has evolved into an intense blur of June filled with individual and team activities that are designed to present opportunities for team and player improvement—and the good programs have players who *commit* to June.

With that in mind, planning an effective summer schedule is vital to the growth of my program. But, I also believe that the mental and physical health of a coach depends on his ability to create a period of time to spend *away* from running his program once the calendar flips to the month of July. Allow me to share some of my thoughts on how I balance a productive *and* healthy summer.

During the summer, none of the basketball activities are *mandatory*; however, players have always been told the truth at Triway and Hoover—a player who fails to commit to his basketball development in the summer will probably have a really tough time finding playing time in the winter, because those who *truly* care can always find the time.

I do *not* pressure our athletes to specialize in one sport, but I *do* want them to find the time within their schedules to work on the game of basketball. Therefore, I feel it is my job to provide myriad opportunities so that our players who participate in other sports have a chance to fit basketball into their schedules. By providing many opportunities, I put the ball in the player's court to make basketball a priority.

When it comes to planning, I make sure we are maximizing program growth during the month of June by sitting down with my staff *in April* and discussing our developmental goals for each grade level. Once we have mapped out our goals, we draw up the June itinerary that offers developmental opportunities for every boy in the North Canton School District—varsity on down through our elementary kids.

At North Canton, we do leave our school campus for a number of events, but the summer program starts right in our own buildings by running our own middle school and high school leagues throughout June.

The high school league is an interesting concept that I developed when I was at Triway, and it has really grown to new heights in my time at Hoover. It's a league that consists of *our* varsity team, a team comprised of Hoover alumni, two teams comprised of players from Walsh University, a team from Malone University, and a team from the University of Mount Union. We don't win many games in this league, but we do learn to compete on a much higher level. I mean, it's real simple: we either learn to get tougher and compete, or we get embarrassed.

In addition to these in-house leagues, I enroll our varsity and junior varsity teams in an outside league to allow the players to play some on their own against other schools. I don't coach my teams in the outside league for a couple of reasons:

First, I believe the summer-league schedule is a good time for my young middle school assistants to coach at the higher levels to get a feel for what varsity action is all about. The second reason that I don't coach in this league is because I feel I can better utilize the ten days the *OHSAA* allots me to work with my team during the summer in other ways. Having the middle school coaches handle the bench during summer league games does not count against those ten days. Running things the way I have explained here has worked out well for my players and staff over the years.

Another big part of our summer experience specific to the varsity level is the weekend shootout events we attend. The weekend events my teams have attended over the years have varied. However, at Hoover we have been attending the *Wheeling Shootout* in West Virginia on a regular basis, and we have also recently included a weekend trip to Wright State University.

On the way home from Wright State we stop for a day in Cincinnati to scrimmage *Moeller High School*—traditionally one of the State of Ohio's top programs. This is usually a great challenge to end the organized part of the summer schedule, and it also allows me to take the players to *King's Island Amusement Park*—which lies just outside of Cincinnati—on the way home. I usually plan this trip so that it takes us to the end of June, and the end of our team schedule.

To go along with the leagues and shootouts, we also run a week-long fundamentals camp for our youth, and at this camp, I require our varsity and junior varsity players to serve as instructors. Having the players instruct the young campers serves two purposes. First, it allows my players the opportunity to strengthen *their* skills and understanding by *teaching*. Second, as the players serve as instructors for the young kids in our community, a bond is formed from our program's present to its future. This bond is another way of developing that strong tradition and continuity that I have mentioned in other segments of the book.

When June ends and we have returned home from our voyage from Wright State to Cincinnati to Kings Island, the kids are usually ready for a break and—more importantly—the coaches are *definitely* ready for a break. According to OHSAA rules, July is a live month for player development, so we *do* continue to provide daily lifting and skill development opportunities on a volunteer basis. But, I also believe it's important to allow the *kids* time to relax, vacation and just be kids. Some of our more serious upper-level players stay on it diligently in July with their skill work or perhaps the AAU trail; some go and do their own thing for a while. Every player is different and—like I said—a rest can be healthy. However, before I take my break I always remind the players that *somewhere someone is always working on his game*. My end of June message is simply meant to encourage them to remember that the *best* players continue to work at it.

For me, July is break time—sort of. I think it's worth mentioning here that being a successful head basketball coach is as much a way of life as it is a profession. And it's not just a way of life for me; it's also a way of life for my wife, Becky. A huge percentage of the things we do are in some way related to basketball—there's no getting around it.

A huge part of a successful summer, to me, is taking some time to do some enjoyable things with Becky—and fortunately for me—Becky loves our life in basketball. An annual foray Becky and I have come to take in July is a "family thing" that is connected to basketball. For many years now, Becky and I have taken a trip to Las Vegas to watch any of my players that might be there for *AAU Nationals*. Prior to the *AAU*

Nationals, I work the *Lebron James Camp* in San Diego, California. Becky usually meets me after the camp and we vacation out west; in fact, it was on one of these excursions that we had one of the greatest experiences of our lives.

One of the true highlights of my life—one I have been able to share with Becky—is getting to know *Coach John Wooden*. We have been to his house many times and spent countless hours getting to know him and his family, and learning about his basketball history. I met Coach Wooden through *Dean Chance*, the 1964 *Cy Young Award* winning pitcher. Dean Chance is from Wooster, Ohio—the town in which Triway is located. Over the course of my head-coaching career at Triway, I got to know Dean very well and we became close friends.

Needless to say, Dean has had an incredible life. Here's a guy who pitched two no-hitters in the big leagues, and in 1964 won his Cy Young Award by posting a 1.65 ERA. In all, Dean Chance pitched 11 shutouts *that year*, was on the cover of *Sport Magazine*, and because he played for the California Angels, was at one point the toast of Hollywood.

Back in 1994, Dean and I were talking when the conversation somehow turned to John Wooden, and I mentioned how much I admired him. I had no idea when I began that conversation with Dean that he was a close friend of Coach Wooden dating back to his days in Hollywood. When he told me he was a friend of the greatest coach of all time, I was impressed; when he promised that he would take me to meet Coach Wooden someday, impressed turned into exhilarated—if not a bit skeptical.

I'm not sure I ever *expected* Dean to follow through on his promise, but a few months later he called my house when I wasn't home and told Becky he was going to LA, and he wanted to take me with him to meet the legendary UCLA coach. When I came home that day, Becky told me about Dean's call. I remember being very excited for the opportunity, and I told Becky how much I wanted to go, but I wasn't sure it would be the smart thing to do. The season is so long that I really hesitate to spend a ton of money on a trip that will take me away from Becky during my down time. Little did I know at the time, but Becky wasn't going to give me any choice.

Knowing how great an opportunity meeting Coach Wooden would be for me, she insisted that I go. When I resisted and told her I really didn't want to leave her in the middle of the summer, she was pleased to hear me say that—it turns out she had already called the airlines to get prices for *our* flight. So *we* did it—*Becky* and I were off to *Beverly Hills* with *Dean Chance* to meet *Coach John Wooden*—a sentence that reminds me how lucky I have been in my life.

We stayed at the Beverly Hills Hilton and met many famous people—and Dean Chance was the ultimate tour guide. The man knew everyone in LA, and he took us to all of the best places Hollywood had to offer. Becky and I enjoyed every second of that first trip, but neither of us enjoyed any of it as much as the time we both spent getting to know John Wooden.

Our visit to Coach Wooden's house was like visiting the Pope. Going in, we hoped to just meet him and say hello. The way it turned out, we ended up staying for six hours and our conversation went far beyond the boundaries of basketball.

After spending all of that time with Coach, we actually found out we had much in common with him. For example, we have a handicapped daughter and he has a handicapped great granddaughter. Family was everything to Coach Wooden, and family is everything to me. It was enjoyable to gain some insight and wisdom from a man who balanced family with basketball while coaching at the highest level. It may seem like this piece of the summer plan has gotten a bit tangential, but my point here is to suggest that creating a good family balance should hold the same importance during the summer as do the actual basketball activities. I just happened to be fortunate enough to gain that perspective from Coach John Wooden!

Of course, Heaven got its new head basketball coach when Coach Wooden passed away during the summer of 2010. But before he joined God's bench, Becky and I went back many times after that first visit and really got to know John Wooden, *the man*. In the end, we came away realizing that at the heart of everything he ever did was the relationship he had with his wife, Nellie. As I said, seeing the importance he placed on his family was a powerful thing.

When something is woven into the fabric of someone's life as much as basketball is woven into mine, basketball and family time often become one and the same. Meeting Coach Wooden was certainly one of those times—a time I shared here because it was one that Becky and I were able to cherish together.

Summer is about basketball *and* family, and it's important to get a mixture of both to maintain a healthy frame of mind. I have been very blessed to be the head basketball coach in two great school districts, and I am blessed even more to have a great family in Becky, and our three lovely daughters: Annie, Erin and Leigh—our severely handicapped angel. As Coach Wooden reinforced, the wife and children of a married coach should be the most important things in his career—as well as the most important things in his life. Having a family that supports and encourages, and truly cares, makes the entire coaching experience more fun. Becky loves basketball, and having a wife that loves basketball and kids who have grown up around the game and love it too, makes the good times more fun and the tough times easier to get through.

100 (Kramer)

Every year I planned the same summer: join the local summer league and play all of the Stark County schools—the area surrounding Canton, Ohio; run a five-day skills camp for the middle school and elementary school kids; offer skill sessions for the high school kids; get in a few shootouts; and go to *The Bob Huggins' Team Camp* at the *University of Cincinnati*. This was what I did, because it was all I ever knew—and it always worked well, because I was always around kids who were varsity ready and would comply with the schedule. Unfortunately for me, the dynamics at Fairless following the 2003 season were different than any I had ever encountered.

Coming off a three-season stretch that saw my teams win a conference championship, finish in second place twice and consistently finish the season ranked in *Ohio's AP Top 10*, the Fairless program had really reestablished a name for itself, especially in Stark County and Northeast Ohio. We were winning, and I was fortunate to have players at Fairless my first couple of years that were willing to devote time in the summer to developing their games and working to become better as a team—just like it was when I was an assistant for Henry Cobb at Canton South High School. I had witnessed nothing but success in my career, so it's easy to understand how I fell into complacency when it came to planning my program's summer.

Unfortunately, while we were enjoying success in my first three seasons at Fairless at the varsity level, the lower levels of the program were struggling—*mightily*. My first year at Fairless saw my seventh graders go 3-13 and my eighth graders complete their two junior high seasons with a combined record of 1-31. At the same time, my ninth graders were turning out a 1-15 season. That's three classes with a combined record of *4 wins and 59 losses*. Three years later, those three classes were seniors, juniors and sophomores, and the success I had always been around had not prepared me to know how to handle what was coming. It was the perfect storm for a disaster.

As the summer of 2003 approached, I did as I had always done. I sent out all of the deposits for all of the shootouts and team camps we had been attending the previous years at Fairless and South. Why not? It had always been good enough. We had graduated *nine* seniors that had been a big part of a very nice two-year run, but *in my mind* the things that had worked in the past would continue to work with no change needed. I was wrong, and I knew it the first weekend in the summer of 2003 when we traveled to play at the *Steubenville Summer Slam Shootout.*

After our three-day varsity/junior varsity mini-camp, we headed to Steubenville with a summer roster that consisted of a number of seniors, one junior, two sophomores, and one talented freshman—a tiny point guard named Jonah Manack, who I mention by name now because he became the foundation upon which the eventual rebuilding was done at Fairless.

Of the seniors, only a player by the name of Mitchell Lambert had ever played any role in the success of the previous seasons and, whereas he was a very good defender and tremendous teammate, he was not going to offer much in the way of replacing the *two thousand points* that had graduated the previous year. The other seniors were very nice kids who had been loyal to the program, and had been positive members of the team, but they were kids who had struggled to compete and win games at the *junior varsity* level for the prior *two* years.

To make matters more difficult, our one junior was a player by the name of Elijah Desmond, a young man who in middle school was on track to have a *world-class career—in wrestling.*

Elijah never intended to pick up a basketball in his life—a point he joked with me about when I was his eighth-grade English teacher my first year at Fairless. However, prior to his entering high school, a doctor diagnosed Elijah with a rare spinal cord defect that made him a very high risk to suffer permanent paralysis by partaking in the everyday contact that wrestling demanded. For the life of me, I can't believe that any doctor ever released him to play *any sport*, but Elijah's doctor released him to participate in a *"non-contact"* sport like basketball. Well, I don't know what basketball game that doctor had been watching over the years, but I'm also not one to argue with a doctor's signature, so Elijah joined the program as a ninth-grader who had never touched a basketball in his life—*literally*.

I never in a million years dreamed that Elijah would last in the basketball program. I just thought that his success as a wrestler would have created a competitive ego that would not allow him to sit on the bench during games while he learned during practice—a concept that has long since been lost in the "me-first" culture in which kids are currently raised. But I was wrong. It was all of Elijah's classmates who had gone 2-48 during their seventh, eighth, and ninth grade seasons that dropped out of the program, and Elijah who persevered and made it as a part-time varsity player by his junior season. Elijah is a great story—one of my favorite players of all time—but the fact that he was fighting for a spot in the rotation as a junior was not a ringing endorsement of the state of the talent level in our program heading into the 2003-04 season.

From the sophomore class, we had two decent players who would have been *far* better served to play a year of junior varsity ball with no exposure to the demands of the varsity game. They both had a chance to become good high school players, but neither really had a skill set that gave his game any identity, and the varsity level is not the best place for a young player to establish such an identity. Ready or not, they were going to play at the varsity level because we didn't have anyone else.

Finally, that brings me back to the one ninth grader we had in our program I felt had the athletic ability and mental makeup to handle the jump to varsity basketball right out of middle school, Jonah Manack. Jonah entered the summer before his ninth-grade season at about 5'7" and 140 pounds, *maybe*. But he had good quickness and an incredible skill set. Jonah could handle the ball adroitly with both hands under pressure; he was a great passer who saw the floor better than any kid I had ever coached to that point in my career; and he had a picture-perfect left-handed jump shot with range that defied his stature. I decided before the summer ever started that Jonah was going to spend four years with me at the varsity level, *through thick and thin*, and I told him exactly that before he ever walked out of eighth grade for the last time. In retrospect, deciding to bring Jonah up and letting him learn at the highest level was the *one* smart thing I did that summer—although it did come at a cost in that playing varsity would negatively affect Jonah's confidence for a period of time because of all the losing he had to endure.

With that crew, we showed up in Steubenville on a Saturday morning in early June of 2003. I had told the Steubenville coach when I registered for the event that we had graduated everyone and might not be in great shape to compete early in the summer, so he assured me that he would take that into consideration when he scheduled.

Sure enough, he set us up in the weakest pool, and—short version of the story—we went 3-2 in five games of pool play on Saturday and Sunday. There was *some* good and *plenty* of bad, but—via a tiebreaker— we qualified for the four-team single-elimination playoff that would take place Sunday evening. As it turned out, we would have been way better off taking the false sense of self 3-2 had given us and gone home with a little confidence and our dignity intact.

Unfortunately, we stuck around for the shootout playoffs, coming out in the first round against a small school by the name of Shadyside— a team that warmed up at the opposite end of the court in Steubenville's historic *St. John Arena* with only *five* players. They had played five games in a thirty-six hour span and had only five players remaining. As I watched the two teams complete warm-ups—certain that a team carrying five players would not have enough left in the tank after five games in two days to beat my roster of ten—I remember thinking how much confidence this new group would gain by making it to the championship game of its first shootout. In that fleeting moment, forgetting that the teams we had beaten in pool play were horrible, the sense of self I had as a coach who could take *any* group of players and be successful was in full bloom—for about ten minutes.

As a frosty night in June is to a rose in full bloom, what happened next knocked the bloom off my coaching rose. Allow me to summarize: Shadyside led *34-2—at halftime*. That ought to make things pretty clear. And if this is even believable—despite the fact that we scored a few more points—the second half looked worse. Honestly, I remember most things that happen to my teams over the years, good and bad, but I truly never looked to see what the final score of that game was. We played one *decent* team in the shootout, and it had beaten us as thoroughly as I had ever been beaten in anything in my life—and they did it with only *five* players, none of whom was Kobe Bryant. At that moment I knew two things: the program was in trouble, and the rest of the summer schedule was not going to be conducive to fixing the problems.

Before we dragged ourselves into the vans to go home, I tried to spin the Shadyside disaster to the kids as a situation where we were just tired, but I could see on the faces of all of the upperclassmen that they weren't really buying it, probably because—for the first time in my coaching career—I didn't really believe in what I was selling. Sure, Jonah and the two sophomores bought it, but the upperclassmen had seen what success looked like up close, and they knew that what went on against Shadyside was unlike anything they'd ever seen.

I believe this was especially difficult on Mitchell Lambert—a player who played significant roles on two outstanding teams as a sophomore and junior. Mitchell was a Fairless kid who had grown up wanting to be a Fairless varsity basketball player, and after that first weekend, he could see his senior season for what it was destined to be—a rebuilding project. Worse, the fact that Mitchell recognized this meant that the other seniors probably did too, and I was afraid that the hopelessness that might ensue could destroy the rest of our summer.

My fears were realized two days later, a Tuesday, at our next individual skill session when none of the seniors—that's exactly *zero*—showed up to participate. Jonah was there as were Elijah, a handful of sophomores, and two of Jonah's ninth-grade classmates who would become instrumental in the renaissance of the program, Brian Cross and Luke Erb—but no seniors.

Although these workouts were not mandatory, I had never coached a group of seniors who *did not want* to participate regularly. So, I called each senior after the workout to see why he had not shown. Each politely gave me a pretty bad excuse, and none would commit to when I might see them again.

The rest of the summer I *would not* see more than one or two seniors at a time—at most workouts, I wouldn't see any of them. It was that summer that taught me this lesson: *A team can never win a December game during the month of June, but a bad June can definitely lose December games.*

The rest of the summer was a disaster. We played in varsity shootouts and summer league games with a makeshift varsity roster oftentimes consisting of a senior or two, the better younger players, and some players who were not even ready to play in *junior varsity* games. The results were brutal on the scoreboard, and although I never think winning and losing is the ultimate judge of a summer game, I do believe it's important to establish competitiveness. Instead, we were establishing hopelessness and the mindset that everyone was plenty better than us—a mindset that ultimately took us the better part of two and half seasons to completely shake.

We ended our summer schedule in 2003 with our annual trip to Cincinnati—a trip not one senior attended. This was a clear sign that not one of them cared to fight through difficult times and try to compete. I was disappointed that they did not want to commit, but I understood on many levels, because they had struggled at every level in the program, and they were never really given much of a chance at the varsity level before that summer. What I was witnessing with those kids also made me realize that I *did not* have a magic wand—no coach does—that I could wave to make every group of kids competitive.

At *The Bob Huggins Team Camp*, a tremendous camp hosted by Coach Huggins every summer, the games were not competitive; with the roster we had there's no way they could have been. But our younger players got a thrill out of playing in the *Shoemaker Center*, and they also thoroughly enjoyed all of the things we did off the floor—including spending a day at *Paramount Pictures King's Island Amusement Park* on the way to the camp. Ironically, what first looked to be the exclamation point on the worst summer of all time *instead* became the springboard for the relationships that would be built within the core of my younger players—relationships that became the foundation upon which the resurgence of our program would be built.

What's the point to sharing stories from a summer of basketball activities that were pretty much a waste of time? Simple: to send the message that a coach must be careful to assess a program before scheduling summer events, because the wrong events can be very destructive to the development of a program. Now, I'm not sure that a better summer plan would have altered the outcome of the 2003-04 season—a season that saw my program struggle through a 3-19 record—but it motivated me to make sure the summer of 2004 would be the best one I had ever planned.

I started the planning by assessing the strengths and weaknesses of the program, then I held *exit interviews* with all of my players who would return for the 2004-2005 season. I made sure to take every variable into account and communicate some very specific objectives to the players.

First variable: personnel. We would return five varsity lettermen from 2003-2004 and none of them would be seniors. There *were* three who would be juniors, the best of which was a lanky 6'2" wing named Kurtis Kuhle—a player who had a strong desire to win and dedicated a lot of time and energy to the program.

Beyond Kurtis' talents, I liked him because he was the lone link to the 2003 team that had won 17 games, finishing second in the conference and in the *AP Top 10*. As a freshman, Kurtis dressed varsity for that team and—although he played sparingly that year—he knew what good basketball looked like. I was hoping he could teach my younger players some of the things that were so abstract to them—like winning *a quarter* or practicing hard—and I felt his experience gave him a chance to be a great leader for two years.

Besides Kurtis and a couple of other juniors who never really distinguished themselves as basketball players, and Elijah—our wrestler turned basketball player and our one senior—the rest of the roster would be made up of three sophomores and four very skilled, albeit very small, ninth graders.

None of the kids mentioned above were even a shade taller than 6'3", and most of them were somewhere around 5'8". But they loved playing basketball with each other, they were all skilled, and they all wanted to be in the gym —all the time. Any coach would have fallen in love with these freshmen and sophomores—Jonah Manack, Luke Erb, Brian Cross, Jordan Jennings, Josh Penland, Garret Manack, and Josh Brinley—because, ladies and gentlemen, these are the kids next door, the ones we all coach. And whereas junior Kurtis Kuhle's physical maturity made him my best player heading into 2004-05, I knew my sophomores and freshmen were the kids that were going to get Fairless back to the top. So, I wanted to make sure my summer gave them the confidence that they could do that.

Second variable: confidence. In assessing the state of the program, I went back in my mind through the previous season and the previous summer, and I realized that *establishing a winning mindset* would be *the* most important thing to do after all the losing we had incurred over the previous twelve months. The thing that made it easier was the fact that my incoming ninth graders were coming off a very successful run at the middle-school level and, whereas that does not always translate to the high school levels, suffice it to say those kids were sure that it would—they were cocky and expected to win. I knew the confidence of my incoming freshmen would not be the problem.

It was my sophomores—Jonah Manack, Luke Erb, and Brian Cross—that I worried about. They were every bit as talented as my incoming freshmen, but they had just spent a season playing for a varsity team to which winning had become a foreign concept. I *preached* to them throughout their freshmen season—through all the losses—that things would be different when they were upperclassmen, but I knew I had to find a way to show them. Therefore, I stepped outside the box to plan the summer of 2004.

Instead of taking my ninth and tenth graders and putting them in a bunch of varsity shootouts with the juniors and one senior we had returning, I first put them in a junior varsity team camp at a local high school where I knew they would be playing against tenth and eleventh graders. I knew it was going to seem odd to my sophomores that I wanted to take them to a junior varsity team camp—only because they had all lettered varsity as freshmen—so I started by selling it to Jonah.

When Jonah Manack bought something, the players in his class and the class below him bought it, too. One of my assistants declared Jonah *"The Godfather of Fairless Basketball"* when he entered his senior year, and it was true. He had that kind of influence as a leader over his classmates and the younger kids, and he ended up using that influence in a very positive manner.

I explained to Jonah that we would attend the junior varsity camp because the state of our program had robbed him and his classmates of the opportunity to experience success by playing a season at that level. I told him that I couldn't change that *during the season*, but I could use part of the summer to give him an abbreviated junior varsity season so that he could see what basketball at Fairless would look like when he and his friends all matured into juniors and seniors. I told him I wanted him to get a chance to go compete against kids his age so he could get his confidence back. Jonah bought every word of my idea and got all of my freshmen and sophomores on board.

So, we went to the four-day junior varsity team camp at Wadsworth High School, *and we smoked everyone*. Sixteen games in four days, and 16-0 was the final record. There was only one game all week that was closer than a ten-point margin, and most of the games were mismatches from the start—not physically; *strictly skill, talent, and basketball IQ*.

After a couple days of experiencing the clinic the Fairless kids were putting on *in every game*, someone began circulating the word that two of our players had lettered varsity the year before, and some opposing coaches started whining a little bit. I found that to be pretty funny, because those coaches who were whining were all carrying juniors on their camp rosters, and I was using three sophomores and five freshmen.

In the end, I honestly didn't care what anyone else thought. We attended that camp to establish a winning mindset in the players that would be critical for our program moving forward, and that's exactly what we accomplished. It was a bit unorthodox, but it was the smartest thing we could have possibly done that summer given the circumstances, and it was critical to the rebuilding of my program at Fairless.

Taking those young varsity players to that junior varsity camp was just one example of adjusting the summer itinerary so that it would reflect the needs of my program. In that case, the adjustment was made to nurture some young players who either had been rushed, or were about to be rushed, to the varsity level out of necessity. It was my way of showing them tangible success—something that I stressed to my players was a foreshadowing of the way things would be when they were juniors and seniors. Having made that adjustment and seeing its positive effects, I began to evaluate some of the other things we had been doing during the summer over the years.

The next thing we decided to do as a staff was to eliminate the *formal* summer league. The summer league began as a concept that was meant to give kids a place to explore their games and develop. But over the years, the summer leagues in which we participated evolved into an extension of the regular season—we were playing the same teams, we were seeing the same officials, the leagues were charging admission at the door, the concession stand was up and running, and the fans and parents were in the stands. Sadly, the local media even occasionally covered a "*big*" summer league game—whatever that means. These leagues became anything but a place a player could develop his game; in fact, players tended to fall back into the same roles in which they had been cast the prior season, because the emphasis was placed back on winning—right down to the single-elimination tournament at the end.

After examining this concept closely, I decided my program would never again pay to play in a formal summer league, because I believed it had become counter-productive. I decided until a better alternative became available, we would scrap paying the $500 to participate in a league and find other ways to spend our time and money more constructively so that our players could expand their games.

From the summer of 2004 through the summer of 2006, we didn't play in any summer league. We met for skill development three times a week during the month of June, and those sessions were directed by our upper classmen. They were very informal sessions that allowed players to work on their skills, then play some five-on-five following the skill work. Also, during those skill sessions in June, we used several of our ten days allowed by the *OHSAA* to work on fine-tuning our system. We simply put out to all players interested in basketball that these sessions would be available to them, and the kids showed up—simple as that. And when they were there, they worked to get better.

The weekends in June were then set aside for traveling to shootouts and team camps. We continued to go to Steubenville the first weekend in June to play in the annual Summer Slam—we stayed in a hotel on Saturday night and made going to *PNC Park* in Pittsburgh to watch a Major League Baseball game an annual team-building event. Besides that annual shootout, we mixed it up and went to a variety of one and two-day shootouts at various locations—but none of them were local.

During the summer, I try not to play anyone we might play during the regular season. I don't even want to see those teams in June. Here's why: If we beat them, we get a false sense of how good we might be in comparison; and if we lose to them, we give our opponents confidence that they can beat us. Also, in-season rivalries are heated enough that they do not need to be stoked by something that might happen in the summer. To me it's a no-win proposition to play teams in the summer we play during the regular season, so I avoid it by staying away from local shootouts.

One thing that I believe strongly in regardless of competitive level is having a culminating summer activity that the players really look forward to. At Fairless we always went to a team camp someplace the kids enjoyed going. After making *The Bob Huggins Team Camp* our culminating experience in the summer for my first three years at Fairless, we started mixing it up. The one year we were too young for the challenges of such a camp, we went to the junior varsity team camp at Wadsworth, so we *did* take one year off from the culminating experience concept. However, the following year we decided to take our trip to West Virginia University in Morgantown to participate in *The John Beilein Team Camp*.

The experience at WVU was tremendous—the accommodations were first class, the competition was excellent, the facilities top-notch—and I have never met a finer man in coaching than Coach Beilein. In fact, Coach Beilein was the reason we decided to go back to Morgantown for a second year. Coach Beilein made his mark at WVU and has since moved into *The Big Ten* at *The University of Michigan*, but I still believe he is one of the most under-rated coaches in the game. His offensive package is an ingenious array of cuts and patterns that—when run correctly—is a thing of beauty to watch. But it is his system of fundamentals, which he shared with the coaches at the camp, that I believe make him one of the best coaches in the country.

The things he teaches are simple and pure basketball movements, but when a player masters them, all of the *nonsense* turnovers that can happen during the course of a game are virtually eliminated. Coach Beilein's teams at WVU were routinely in the top five in the country at ball security, so I took the opportunity to learn from the best and began to incorporate what I now call "Beilein Fundamentals" in my system. And Coach Beilein was very engaging and visible at the camp, but here is a little story that made me one of his biggest fans:

One of my players, Luke Erb, had been elbowed in the mouth at a shootout at *Mount Union College* two weeks prior to the WVU trip. The elbow knocked five of Luke's teeth out at the root, and we literally had to pick them up off the floor and take Luke to a local hospital where emergency oral surgery was performed to preserve his teeth. Had that been me who took that elbow, I wouldn't have been playing two weeks later, but Luke was a tough kid and he was playing with a protective mouth guard.

One afternoon at the camp, Coach Beilein just happened to decide to sit down and have lunch in the cafeteria with my staff and me— another reason I am a huge fan of his. As he was talking basketball and we were listening, Luke Erb came over to our table to tell me that he had left his special mouth guard on his tray and accidentally thrown it out. He had tried to dig through the garbage to find it, but it was gone. When Coach Beilein heard the type of mouth guard Luke needed, he knew that his trainers had some in stock, but that the mouth guards were over at the Coliseum—about a two-mile drive from the cafeteria.

Coach Beilein never hesitated. He asked me when our next sched-uled game was and he promised us he would drive to the Coliseum himself and bring Luke back a mouth guard so he could play in that game. He could have put it on one of his student assistants and *never* even checked to see if it had gotten done, but—twenty-five minutes after lunch ended—Coach Beilein himself walked into the recreation center where our next game was ready to begin and handed Luke Erb that mouthpiece. I was highly impressed to see that a big-time college coach was thoughtful enough to do that—especially for a 5'6" kid with no chance of playing college basketball. We loved going to Morgan-town, because it was a great camp and Coach Beilein is simply as good as it gets.

As I said earlier, we also like to mix it up and keep it fresh, and we really went over the top in the summer of 2007. I've alluded to this night a number of times and will continue to do so, because it was the greatest night I have ever been able to share with my players, coaches, family and friends in my coaching career: On March 10th, 2007, we won the *Canton Division-II District Championship* by defeating two-time defending state runners-up Wooster Triway in a game that featured *the most dramatic ending* I am ever likely to experience as a coach—again, more on the ending later.

By winning the *District Championship*, the *third* in the *sixty-year* history of Fairless basketball, Jonah, Jordan Jennings and all of the key characters from those early rebuilding days had elevated the program to new heights. Those kids had put Fairless on the map of elite Division-II basketball programs in the State of Ohio, and a good number of the players were only juniors, meaning we would be returning a very talented and experienced team for the 2007-2008 season. I knew this meant that careful planning of the ensuing summer would be crucial to keeping the interest of the players who had played their last three tournament games in front of crowds in excess of 5,000 fans. I knew it would take something special to avoid a letdown.

I decided I wanted to reward the returning players for the commitment they had shown the program and the success they had achieved while presenting them with the biggest challenges we could find in the way of competition. We would do the *Steubenville Summer Slam* again, because the kids enjoyed the team-building activities we annually did on that trip with the hotel and the night out in Pittsburgh at a Pirates' game; we also went to a shootout at The College of Wooster that boasted some pretty good teams from various parts of Ohio; and we played in what is now termed an "Open Gym League" invented by legendary Dover coach, Bob VonKaenel—a league that carried no fees, no officials, no standings, and no fans. It was pure basketball—all about competition in a structured open-gym setting. And whereas all of those things fit well together with our regular morning individual work, the culminating activity was the thing that kept everyone focused—a trip to *The University of North Carolina at Chapel Hill* to play twelve games in the storied *Dean Smith Center*.

Hey, playing on the court where Jerry West played at *WVU* was a thrill; and playing on the main court where all of Coach Huggins' great teams played so many big games at the *University of Cincinnati* was also certainly a memorable experience for the players. However, playing in the *Dean Smith Center* on the campus of *The University of North Carolina at Chapel Hill* provided a memory of a lifetime for my players—which was the main goal for deciding to attend that camp.

At the *UNC Team Camp* everything was first class. There were six teams in the field that had either won their state title or were state runners-up the prior season; the dorm where we stayed had nice rooms—as far as dorms go—and there was an outdoor swimming pool for the players to enjoy. The food was good and plentiful; and, as advertised, we played every game in the Smith Center—a true shrine to the game of basketball.

At the camp, the team played well against terrific competition, qualifying for the *gold tournament*, which included the best eight teams in the field. We finished fifth—for what it's worth—but it was all of the other things that made the trip so special. One of the really neat things about this camp was that Coach Roy Williams, his staff, and his players were all highly visible and extremely accommodating the three days we were there. Over the years I have gone to a number of camps and never have I been to one where the players in that program were more impressive in the way they helped run the camp. From the North Carolina player nobody would ever recognize to Tyler Hansborough, *the 2008 National Collegiate Player of the Year*, they were terrific to us. In fact, Tyler Hansborough actually kept the clock and scoreboard during four of our games, and not a more polite young man have I ever met. The trip—to pull a phrase out the 1980's—was simply awesome.

We took video, lots of pictures to give to the players as keepsakes, and we even took our white game uniforms on the trip to wear during the last day so that we could have a team picture taken on the famous State of North Carolina logo at center court in the Smith Center. I truly believe that we *did* create memories together on that trip that will last a lifetime, and it reinforced in the minds of our players and the people associated with our program at Fairless that being a Fairless basketball player was a special privilege.

In the last several pages I have given quite a few details on some of the summer activities my teams have participated in at different developmental stages. Again, the point to this is to show that I believe deeply in making sure the summer experiences we partake in mesh with the competitive abilities of the players at a given time. In other words, *the best-laid plans* must be adapted from year to year if they are to *always* be *the best-laid plans*.

In 2004, we needed to find a place to let our young kids get some confidence, so we went to a junior varsity camp at Wadsworth High School; in 2007 we were coming off of a "*Sweet-16*" appearance with a good core of returning players, so we went to the *University of North*

Carolina at Chapel Hill to play the best competition we could find in one of the great college basketball arenas in the nation. Although hundreds of miles away from each other and worlds apart in basketball lore, both camps—along with all of the other things we do to help our players develop over the summer—were essential in the process of rebuilding Fairless into a successful basketball program.

Today, when I start planning a summer, I draw on the good and bad experiences I have had in the past, but I also seek the advice and expertise of Randy Montgomery. One of the things Randy does is run his own league for Hoover players, and he brings back alumni and college players to give his kids great competition. Whereas I have never been the head coach of a program at a developmental stage to play against college players, I adapted Randy's idea to fit my program when I was at Canton South. I called it the Developmental League, or D-League.

I set the D-League up to be played in eight sessions on Mondays and Wednesdays throughout the month of June, and we used the meetings as part of the ten instructional days the *OHSAA* allows a varsity staff to work with the players.

Each session of our D-League began with a thirty-minute skill segment followed by a thirty-minute team segment, which I used to install and adjust our system for the upcoming season. To me, the first hour is the most important aspect of these sessions, because it allowed us to help players develop their fundamentals and learn the "South Way" of playing basketball. The last hour of each session—league play—was for the players to have some fun and build some chemistry and team leadership.

For league play, each team started with a senior as its captain, and the seniors then drafted his players before the first session. Each team played two, twenty-minute games per session, and we had a single-elimination tournament the final day of the D-League to determine a champion.

The champions of the D-League did receive some t-shirts, but the point to this league was certainly not to give away prizes—*the point to the league was to help the players develop and to give each young man an opportunity to compete against other South players so that we as a staff could evaluate the players and get a better idea of where each would best be placed for the ensuing season.*

Since I really liked the idea of the Developmental League, I instituted D-Leagues at the middle school and elementary levels as well—same format: skill segment; team segment; games. The biggest difference at the lower levels is that more time was spent on the fundamental segment, and the team segment was far more basic.

For the small fee we charge for the league, the players at the younger levels received a reversible D-League jersey and a *"MagicCats"* basketball. The "MagicCats" ball afforded each boy in the D-League a free admission into our "MagicCats" little dribblers program—another developmental concept for the youth in my program that starts in the summer.

The "MagicCats" ball-handling program is my program's version of the "Wizards" and "Hoopsters" programs that have been such a huge part of Coach Montgomery's programs at Triway and Hoover. I have seen the success of Coach Montgomery's programs at Triway and Hoover, and I have listened to him talk about how these little dribbler programs have been such a vital part of it, so I decided to make it a part of my program at Canton South.

Like Coach Montgomery said when he wrote about the Wizards and the Hoopsters, this program will connect the present to the past; it will go a long way toward building tradition; and it will put the parents of these young boys in the seats to watch them perform at halftime of varsity games during the season. All of the things the "MagicCats" little dribblers program has to offer are positive, and the kids and their parents loved it.

Putting together a summer plan that will benefit the growth of my entire program while preparing the varsity team for the next season is one of the most important roles I serve as a head coach. To do so effectively I must first put developmental activities in place in my home gym that will ensure the basics of our system are being taught in an environment my staff can control. Second, I must make sure that the events in which we partake outside of our gym meet the competitive needs of our program.

Like most aspects of creating *the best-laid plans* for running a program, the summer philosophy under which I now operate has evolved over the years. Of course, I'm not sure a summer plan can ever be considered perfect but, through trial and error and with the help of a close friend in the likes of a 500-win coach, I am comfortable knowing that the summers I plan will always be productive.

11

A Brief Look at X's and O's:

Trial & error; multiple looks; run & stun

500

AS COACH KRAMER stated in the book's introduction, *The Best-Laid Plans of a High School Basketball CEO* is not a book geared toward *X's & O's*. However, because a head coach's basketball acumen is certainly important, I will *address* the *X's & O's* as I have other aspects of the job. The first thing to remember is that there are a lot of ways to play the game of basketball, so rather than giving information about *specific X's & O's*, I will approach the topic by sharing the manner in which my system has evolved.

As I look back through my three decades as a head coach, I have found that much of what I consider to be *the best-laid plans* on the basketball court has come about through trial and error—and I would suggest to any young head coach to go the same route in developing his on-floor philosophy. I believe in reading as much good literature written by other coaches on leadership and running an organization as I can, but I'm not huge on reading a lot of books on strategy, patterns and other ideas related to *X's & O's*. Why? I think those things can be confusing.

When someone writes a book or gives a clinic, that coach is usually giving the audience a shell of the knowledge it takes to effectively teach a team to run his offense or defense. Remember, the coach on the forty-five-minute video has spent a career getting to the point where he is having enough success with his offense or defense to market a video. Knowing this, no coach should ever think watching that video gives him the ability to teach its contents to his team so that the team is capable of *effectively* executing it with any aptitude. It's just not possible.

There are some great coaches out there who can give a terrific presentation on DVD or at a clinic on their offenses and make them look unstoppable, and I'm not knocking that at all. However, what a young coach needs to understand is this: Once he has watched that video a hundred times, the trial and error part has just begun, because that video cannot possibly contain an answer to all of the 'what-ifs' a basketball game presents. If a coach at the high school level decides to jump and teach the new trendy offense of the latest "hot" coach, he better be ready to reach out to try to contact other coaches who effectively run that offense—and likewise be ready to spend an awful lot of time seeking and watching the game film of teams who are running it—because there's plenty more to every offense than what a person can garner from watching a forty-five-minute presentation.

With that in mind, when young coaches ask me about choosing an offense and defense to install, I always suggest that they start with a *simple* offensive and defensive philosophy, and build the entire system around that by letting things evolve. Each year will be different as personnel changes, but installing some basic structures that can be mastered and executed by all personnel will keep a coach from having to change everything at the beginning of each season. Here's the way I look at it: If my opponents are continuously changing their offense every year while my program stays in the same base system every year, my teams will be far better capable of executing our offense because of the experience factor. Common sense tells me kids will run an offense with a much higher aptitude after being in that offense for two, three or four years than the teams who have been running their offense for twelve practices.

At the defensive end of the court, I always begin teaching with man-to-man principles. I do not feel a team can be good at *any* defense until man-to-man concepts have been taught. I have utilized a variety of defenses over the years and had success with quite a number of them. However, I always start with man-to-man principles and our defensive schemes evolve from there through the season.

I actually like to have as many as ten different defensive schemes, because having a variety of schemes on hand allows me to make in-game adjustments, and it also allows me to have some things ready to go for the tournament that can be used to surprise even the most prepared opponent. Some teams are capable of handling more schemes than others, so knowing personnel and allowing things to evolve from season to season are important concepts to embrace.

On the offensive end of the floor I always begin by teaching an open-post offense that can be adapted later to other offensive concepts. Again, personnel will dictate *what* and *how much* we do offensively, but I have always started with the open-post cut and fill concept. Within the open-post offense, many fundamentals must be taught which will develop the players and ultimately make them understand the game. This offense and its in-depth concepts were taught to me by Ed McCluskey from Farrell, Pennsylvania, Charlie Huggins from Indian Valley High School, and Bob Huggins.

When I coached with Bob Huggins at Walsh College, we implemented this offense and he was a true master at breaking it down daily in order to effectively teach it. The name Bob Huggins continues to show up in this book because the man can just flat out coach. The reason I stop to praise him again here is because our teams at Walsh always got better offensively and defensively as a season progressed, and the open-post offense was a reason for both.

The offense is pure basketball: cutting, passing, setting and reading screens. As the offense improved executing all of these basketball movements, the defense had no choice in practice but to get better at defending them. A team mastering the fundamentals of offense and defense at the same time is the *perfect* practice scenario—and Bob Huggins was the master at it. Working with Bob allowed me to see the benefits to this, so I have tried to emulate his example in my practices over the years.

Besides offense and defense, the other concept that I think is worth mentioning here is *tempo*. Tempo is an extremely important concept in the game of basketball and controlling it is a strategy in and of itself. To me, there are four basic ways to control or dictate tempo:

1.   An offense can speed up the game by fast breaking.

2.   An offense can slow tempo by spreading the floor with good ball handlers.

3.   A defense can press and trap full-court to quicken the pace.

4.   A defense can sag in half-court or extended defenses to slow the pace.

Within the framework of those four concepts, there are an infinite number of strategies for a skilled coach to manipulate the tempo—diamond press; four-corners offense; fast break; 2-2-1 three-quarter court zone; sagging man-to-man; run & jump—the possibilities really are endless.

In my coaching career I have had many teams of varying strengths so, from year to year, a person watching one of my teams might see us playing at any and all speeds. Each coach must decide what tempo makes *him* comfortable, because some coaches just do not trust an up-tempo approach. There's nothing wrong with that; in fact, many great coaches have gotten the job done playing a very deliberate pace. My point here is that it all works when taught effectively—and knowing that it all works makes me comfortable with adjusting tempo to fit my personnel, just as I would adjust my offenses and defenses.

Earlier in this section I made the point that I always suggest to young coaches who ask me about selecting an offense and defense to start with simplicity on both sides of the ball and build from there. Here's the reason I make that suggestion and caution them to stay away from the lore of the trendy new approach: A coach's inability to effectively teach the players to master the fundamentals needed to be successful in a chosen offensive or defensive concept is the equivalent of preparing his players to fail. Similarly, a coach who lacks *depth in his understanding* of an offense or defense in turn lacks the ability to make necessary adjustments when an opponent has found an effective way to counter.

The game can get complicated if a coach isn't careful, and that's why I always start with simplicity and familiarity on both ends of the floor—then I allow things to evolve from there.

100 (Kramer)

I played for two coaches in my basketball career and both preferred trying to win low-scoring games with physical man-to-man defense and a very methodical offense. Having played that style of ball and seeing how it worked exceedingly well for my college coach, Steve Moore at *The College of Wooster*, early in my career I approached preparing my teams to play a similar style.

Further contributing to my defense-first approach was the fact that my first experience as an upper-level assistant came with Henry Cobb, a man who for over a decade was *deservedly* known as a defensive guru throughout Northeast Ohio. I have never seen anyone work the defensive end of the floor like Henry Cobb—his meticulous attention to the perfection of every detail made scoring against his half-court defense a nightmare for his opponents. Ironically, working *for* Henry Cobb, then having to coach *against* him, went a long way toward shaping the system of play I am teaching today. I say *ironically* because my offensive approach has evolved into the polar opposite of the system Coach Cobb used all those years.

Coach Henry Cobb was great at teaching man-to-man defense as his base defense, but he was also a multiple-looks coach at the defensive end. Whereas the man-to-man defense his South teams played was always solid, Coach Cobb specialized in implementing a *1-2-2 match-up zone* that became nearly impossible to penetrate by the time his teams perfected it the second part of a season. Coach Cobb rode his 1-2-2 match-up zone to four district titles and a trip to the *Final Four* in his fifteen years at Canton South.

I mention Coach Cobb's success for two reasons: first, beside my father and Randy Montgomery, no coach has been more influential in my coaching career than Henry Cobb; second, having to try to prepare my teams to score against his defenses forced me to become an innovative *offensive* coach.

Of course my first efforts at coaching to attack Henry Cobb's defenses came while I was his junior varsity coach for seven years at Canton South, where it was my job to challenge his defenses with my junior varsity players during practice—a nearly impossible feat. I had terrific *junior varsity* players every year I coached with Henry Cobb at Canton South, but South was a dominant program during my time with him because of great defense. Therefore, there were days early in my stint as his junior varsity coach when my kids *couldn't so much as get a shot off* in a fifteen-minute segment of practice against his defense.

Watching that got really old from where I stood, and it was awfully frustrating for my young players as well, so I started to create wrinkles out of Coach Cobb's base offense to help my players get some looks at the basket. Some of those wrinkles didn't work, but I was pleased to find that many of them did. Whether my junior varsity players were facing his man-to-man or his 1-2-2 match-up, I had something ready. At first it irritated Coach Cobb, because he thought I was trying to break from his concept, but I continued to explain that I was simply trying to give my guys a chance to compete and push his varsity players. I'm sure *I* was annoying on some levels, but somewhere along the line Coach Cobb decided that what I was doing was good for the program for a couple reasons.

First off, if something was working for my junior varsity team against his defense, there was a pretty good chance it would work against *any* defense, so he started allowing me to add some of my ideas to his offensive system. Just as importantly, it forced the varsity defenders to counteract a variety of different movements—this was especially helpful when they were trying to perfect the 1-2-2 match-up zone, because that zone gets better and better the more experience it gets with different cuts, screens and overloads.

The more I had a chance to play chess with the varsity defense in practice, the more of a taste I got for studying offense. I was still working my players at the defensive end of the floor, but I was constantly watching, studying and consuming all I could about offensive basketball. Like most coaches, I watched all the film I could watch, always with a legal pad in my lap ready to take notes when I found something I liked. And I didn't just watch high school film. I taped college and pro games, and broke those down, too. I couldn't get enough offense.

In my last year on Coach Cobb's staff at Canton South, he offered me the opportunity to move up from the junior varsity level to become his varsity assistant. After six years with Henry Cobb, our relationship had changed—instead of being the young coach who he almost needed to treat like another player, I sensed he had developed a respect for the work I had become capable of doing for him. With that respect, I also sensed he came to trust me enough to let me coach *his varsity players*. I always appreciated Coach Cobb for that. He was an "old-school", hardcore, defensive coach who did not necessarily want to delegate a whole lot of any of the decision-making to anyone else at either end of the court, but he came to delegate some major responsibility for the offensive end of the floor to me.

Truth be told, Henry Cobb and I made a great team. After I had spent some years with him on his staff, he once kidded with me by saying that he felt I would like to try to beat people 110-107. I kidded him back by saying that he'd like to beat people 32-29—then I told him we ought to put our heads together and beat people 110-29. I'm not suggesting Henry Cobb *needed* me to earn *any* of his 400 career wins, because he certainly would have done just fine without me. I'm just saying our strengths complemented each other well—a point that is also relevant to the section about choosing a coaching staff—and coaching with Henry Cobb certainly shaped my thinking at the offensive end of the floor. Hence, I have always been grateful for my opportunity to work with Coach Henry Cobb.

When I left Coach Cobb's staff to take the head-coaching job after the 1999-2000 season to take the job as head coach at Fairless High School, Henry Cobb continued to shape my offensive coaching philosophy—from then on *as my opponent*.

In the final game of my first year at Fairless, Canton South came to our gym for the season finale. We prepared all week to play against Coach Cobb's match-up 1-2-2, because that's the defense South had been using as it rode an extended winning streak into the game. We had enjoyed a nice season, but South was a team that was on a roll and headed places with its 6'4" sophomore point guard Ronnie Bourquin, the area's leading 3-point shooter Jerry Prestier, and a surrounding cast of players who could hurt a team in a lot of different ways. I felt we might be able to pull the upset because we had overcome a number of obstacles to overachieve in the eyes of many, and I also felt my knowledge of how to attack Henry's 1-2-2 would give us an offensive advantage that their other opponents didn't enjoy. Early in the game, it appeared I was correct about that advantage.

On our second offensive possession of the game, I used an offensive wrinkle that was designed to get my best 3-point shooter an open look on the left wing and it worked to perfection—right down to the made shot that put us ahead 3-2.

I sensed that the success of my initial call gave my players confidence our plan to get into the open windows of that zone would work— just as I had sold it to them all week. Unfortunately, I never found out if the next wrinkle would work, because we never saw that zone again.

After one possession in his signature zone defense, Coach Cobb decided not to play around with us. He had bigger, quicker, more physical players, and he decided to find out how we would like *his* defenders right up in *our* faces the rest of the night. The answer was simple: we didn't like it much at all.

South went on a *30-7* run the rest of the half and at the intermission we trailed 32-10. My first Fairless team played some good basketball against some good teams in nearly winning our conference in 2000-2001, but the only thing close we had seen to the South defense was the intensity Coach Montgomery's undefeated Triway Titans had brought earlier in the year. We had not been up to the Triway task back in January, and we weren't up to the Canton South challenge that night.

There was no shame in falling short against those teams: South went on to win the 2001 *Canton Division-II District Championship* and made it to *Ohio's "Elite 8"*; Triway, under Coach Montgomery, went 22-0 and won the Division-II AP State Poll Championship before losing to

South in the *District semi-finals*. But that night against South *did* make me begin to rethink my offensive philosophy—and my next close encounter with a Henry Cobb defense was the push that sent me in search of some permanent improvements.

It was a year later in the semi-finals of the Canton Division-II District where that next encounter occurred. I had a terrific 17-win team at Fairless that had put up big scoring numbers all year long—until we faced Canton South.

In front of one of the biggest crowds in the history of the *Canton Memorial Field House*, Coach Cobb's defense killed our offense by cutting off its head. Here's what I mean: Our offense was very reliant on our point guard to get us into our sets and patterns. Whereas he was a solid player who had done a terrific job all year, Josh Abrigg was not necessarily a natural point guard, and South had the type of on-ball defender that just flat out made him miserable all night long by forcing him into places he didn't want to be on the floor. Therefore, we were running our offense at distances from the basket that made it very difficult to get our tremendous scoring wings good shots. We *had been* a very fluid, free-flowing offensive team all year, but that night was painful to watch.

As the 2002 District semi-final unfolded, it was actually very difficult for South to score, too. We trailed by nine at halftime, but we cut the lead to one early in the fourth quarter and had possession of the ball with a chance to take the lead. In the end, our lack of ability to consistently get good looks at the basket cost us that game.

South beat us 47-38, and it was my fault. I saw how much we struggled the year before against Coach Cobb's style of defense and I ignored the fact that the scheme might have been partially to blame. Going into the 2002 game, I thought that our improved talent would be the difference-maker—and it was true—we did have two terrific wing players that could really fill it up from behind the arc.

However, in assessing our advantage on the wing, I had unintentionally ignored the fact that we were at a distinct disadvantage at the point guard position. In the end, our advantages on the wing didn't matter, because we couldn't consistently get the wings involved. In retrospect, it was an understandable mistake for me to make, because no team had been able to disrupt Josh Abrigg all season long; however, that night the defense played by South's freakishly athletic 6'4" All-Ohio point guard, Ronnie Bourquin—an athlete that went on to fame as a baseball player at Ohio State before being drafted in the second round by the Detroit Tigers—on my point guard was the difference in the game. I realized that night—in the time it took me to walk from the bench to the locker room to say goodbye to my team—I would need to make adjustments in my system if we were ever going to win a game of that magnitude.

I knew when I took the job at Fairless that making a *"Sweet-16" by winning the prestigious Canton Division-II District* meant being able to beat Canton South and Triway in the district tournament. So after the loss in 2002—which made me 0 for 2 against my mentor—I began to search for an offensive concept that would allow my team to function at a high level against a defense like South's, even in the absence of a dominant point guard.

This does not mean I discarded everything in my system in search of the *Holy Grail* of basketball offenses. I liked much of what we were doing at the offensive end of the floor, because it was yielding solid success against most opponents. However, South had stopped my teams cold—twice—and I felt there had to be something out there that would help make the next time different. So, I searched and studied and watched film.

The first offensive concept I came across that fit my needs was *The Triangle Offense*, made famous by Phil Jackson and Tex Winter with the Chicago Bulls and Los Angeles Lakers. I liked the fact that *The Triangle* uses a two-guard front that provides alignment and spacing that makes it nearly impossible for defenses to deny the multiple entries that facilitate the offense. I also had always been enamored with the way those Bulls and Lakers teams seemed to play with such harmony and selflessness.

So I purchased Tex Winter's book *The Triple Post Offense* and all of Coach Winter's videos, and went to work. Once I felt I had a handle on the basic movements of the offense, I began taping Lakers games so I could break the film down and see how the players adjusted to different situations presented by a defense. I absolutely loved every aspect of *The Triangle*, except one: I wasn't sure I had a good enough grasp of all of its nuances to install it so that my players could master it.

In his section on *X's & O's*, Coach Montgomery cautions the readers to beware of jumping into the fad offense while aborting everything else, because it's very difficult to teach an offense as thoroughly as it needs to be taught after watching a few videos and reading a book. Knowing that I liked *The Triangle Offense* and that it was much more than a fad, but also sensing that I did not have the expertise to teach it with the same depth as the man who invented it, I decided I would take pieces of it—like the two-guard front and its array of entries—and incorporate those pieces into *my* system.

Another problem with teaching it is that a high school coach does not get nearly as much time with his players as an NBA coach gets with his, so I figured if my players couldn't master *The Triangle* in its entirety, then I would teach them the parts I felt the players could master. Therefore, some *Triangle concepts* have become a permanent part of *my* offensive system.

Next, I began studying Pete Carrill's *Princeton Offense* for three reasons: first, because I liked the fact that it also starts with a two-guard alignment; second, because it offers a number of ways to hit an over-playing defense with some back-door cuts that result in lay-ups; and third, because a team does not need a big low-post threat to be successful playing in the *Princeton concept*.

I started by going out and buying Coach Carrill's book, *The Smart Take from the Strong*, then I ordered all of the videos in the series he offers the public. I studied and studied the *Princeton Offense* and fell in love with it—just as I had with *The Triangle*. And—just as was the case with *The Triangle*—I worried that my lack of experience with the offense would make it difficult for me to teach all of its nuances so that my players could master it. So, I did exactly what I did with *The Triangle*: I took pieces of *Princeton* that I thought fit my needs and incorporated those pieces into my system.

At this point, it should be easy to see where I'm headed with this. Like Coach Montgomery suggested in his section, a coach's system ought to evolve as he gains experience, and mine was evolving. Some people see my teams today and tell me they like the way we run the *Princeton Offense*. In truth, saying that we run *Princeton* is not accurate, because it is not the offense that Coach Carrill has taught for so many years. What a person sees when he sees my teams play at the offensive end is a *Princeton concept* meshed with some *Triangle concept*, meshed with a number of things I have always done; hence, over the years my offense has become *my* offense.

At Fairless, we called it the *Fairless Offense*; at Canton South we called it the *South Offense*. The most important thing is not its brand name; the most important thing is that I am able to teach it to my players with a level of expertise that allows them to master it. Coupled with the running game my system institutes, my offensive approach has made my teams very difficult to scout and guard.

As Coach Montgomery also mentioned in his section, tempo is a very important factor in developing a system. Refocusing on the goal of trying to beat *a Canton South* or *a Triway* in my days at Fairless, I knew I had to create a style of play that would give my team an identity that would give us an advantage. Canton South had a period of years where they had big, strong and athletic players; Triway took two straight trips to the state title game with players of similar stature. At Fairless, our post players were a shade over 6'2" and most of our guards were all in the 5'7" to 5'10" range. I came to the conclusion that we were never going to beat those types of teams with the guard-oriented player I typically coached at Fairless if we continued to try to stand toe-to-toe with them and slug it out at *their* pace. So I decided I would teach my players to establish *our* pace—which became known as *Run & Stun* in our formidable seasons at Fairless.

In all actuality, *Run & Stun* was born out of the simple desire to commit to playing at a *Phoenix Suns' pace* so that we could avoid always having to go toe-to-toe with the teams who were likely to bludgeon us in a half-court game. I had always liked our running game and my teams had always been pretty good at running when opportunities presented themselves, but this would be different. We were going to start attacking the second we gained possession of the ball—on makes and misses. And our shooters who had worked so hard to master their skills—which is to say every player on the team—were going to launch 3-point shots whenever they could get a look at the basket. *Run & Stun* was simply an all-out commitment to our fast break. The players loved it, and the brand name looked good on the back of a t-shirt.

Of course this sounds simple, but like any other aspect of basketball, it needed to be studied and perfected through teaching its fundamentals. It does very little good to play fast if the players in the system are not capable of making plays playing fast. As we began to commit to the up-tempo game, I had some drills of my own that I had always used to teach it, but I didn't think I had enough to make sure my players were getting full development in the running game. So—just like I did when I was developing my half-court offense—I went out and studied the best coaches I could find relative to the running game.

At the time, there was no coach better at teaching the running game than the Phoenix Suns' Mike D'Antoni, and I wanted badly to watch him work. Two problems: I didn't have access to Coach D'Antoni, and I didn't have two-time *NBA Most Valuable Player Steve Nash* directing my fast break. I solved the problems by focusing on what I *did* have: two *Nash-like* little guards—albeit both left-handed—who could do amazing things in the open court against other high school players, and access to Coach Donnie Jones, the Marshall University Men's Basketball Coach, who is a disciple of coach D'Antoni.

Donnie Jones became Marshall's head coach in 2007 after spending the prior two years as Coach Billy Donovan's assistant at Florida—seasons that saw Coach Donovan's teams win back-to-back National Championships by playing at a break-neck pace. Knowing that Coach Jones was going to install a similar style of play at Marshall, I jumped at the opportunity to travel to Huntington, West Virginia to watch him instruct practice, and pick up on some of the drills and teaching points he used to develop the break-neck pace that made the *Phoenix Suns* and *Florida Gators* championship caliber teams.

The message here to all coaches is that there's *always* a way to learn from the best, and after watching Coach Jones run several practices, I felt I had been connected to the best of the best when it came to the running game. When I left Marshall to return to Stark County, I was confident that I had found the missing pieces I needed to teach the running game at a high level.

The next step in making *Run & Stun* full go was getting the players to believe that I really *did* want them to play *that* fast and take *those* shots in transition. Hey, I won't lie: I was a coach that liked to stand up and call a set play and scheme the ball to the man *I* wanted to get the next shot—and I think there's still a place for that in my system. But when we were operating at our optimum level in our back-to-back great years at Fairless in 2007 and 2008, we would go full quarters without my ever calling a play. Heck, we'd go full quarters without ever getting into our half-court offense. The reason: We became so adept at getting good shots in our running game that it was impossible for some teams to force us into needing to run our offense.

Playing our *Run & Stun* style of basketball forced me to relinquish a lot of the control that most coaches are not comfortable relinquishing, but it worked for me, and our players and fans loved it. I think in the end, the most important thing is that the style of play a coach chooses to use works for him and his players. And one needs to look no further than our tournament run in March of 2007 to see that *Run & Stun* worked for my program.

After winning a double overtime opening round game against Marlington High School and a second round game against a 17-win

Alliance High School team, we were staring at having to beat Canton South in the District semi-finals and Triway in the District Championship Game. There they were: the two programs that I knew we would have to overcome if we were ever to become an elite basketball program at Fairless.

Canton South, of course, presented the challenge of scoring against its vaunted half-court defense; Triway posed the problem of having to deal with size disadvantages all over the floor, including the daunting task of defending the Titan's 6'10" center, Sebastian Weber, who had simply murdered us the first two times we had lost to them that season during conference play.

I'll give the short version of the story on the South game: We knocked Canton South out in the semi-final round by running past them just enough to outscore them in a low-scoring game. It was obviously a huge victory for our program in overcoming one of the area's top programs on such a big stage, but I was a long way past making any game personal in my career, so I took no extra delight in beating my former mentor.

When it comes to the game that followed the South game, however, I simply cannot pass up the opportunity to share what was, without question, one of the most dramatic endings in the history of any high school championship game—ever. Hyperbole? Maybe. I admittedly can be overly enthusiastic about my teams, so I'm finally going to share what happened on March 10th of 2007 in the Canton Division-II District Championship Game at the Canton Memorial Field House, and let the audience decide:

Trailing most of the game by anywhere between five to nine points, my All-Ohio junior guard, Jordan Jennings—the fiery young man characterized in my section on discipline—almost single-handedly wiped out an eight-point deficit on an array of shots in the last minute and twenty seconds of the fourth quarter that included two of the longest three-point goals anyone will ever see a high school player take, much less make. The second one—a pull-up three-pointer from twenty-eight feet on the right wing—tied the game with fourteen seconds on the clock and ultimately sent the game into overtime.

Now, wiping out an eight-point deficit in a little more than a minute of play was dramatic, but more gratifying was the fact that we had learned from our failure to remain composed a month earlier against Triway and made the comeback against our nemesis on an even bigger stage. And as for sheer drama, the best was to follow.

Tied in overtime with 9.9 seconds remaining, we committed a foul on a Triway player who was driving to the basket, putting him on the line for two free throws—the first of which he calmly made as 5,000 fans created high school basketball's version of *March Madness.*

As the Triway player lined up his second free throw, I remember standing at the other end of the court wishing I had a timeout left to call. As it turned out, it was far better that I didn't have any left. For seventy-two practices over a five-month period we had practiced this situation with the goal always being to gain possession and score in nine seconds or less. *Run & Stun* had put us in a position to get where we were that night, and it also put us in the best position to get us the shot we wanted to win the game in just less than ten seconds—without the timeout.

So when the second free throw rebounded long and we gained possession along the right baseline, with no timeouts and holding the ball about ninety feet from the basket, we had the Triway defense right where we wanted it—retreating and scrambling to find our two '*Nash-like*' sharpshooters, Jonah Manack and Jordan Jennings, in transition.

As the play unfolded, my terrific 6'1" forward, Josh Penland, retrieved the long rebound and quickly made an outlet pass to Jonah Manack. Jonah, who had scored 24 points in regulation, took a couple dribbles across half court and immediately drew two defenders. I'm sure he was looking for Jordan Jennings on the right wing, but Jordan was being face-guarded by a Triway defender, so he passed it back to Josh Penland, who trailed him across half court. Penland quickly spotted the man Triway had lost in transition, senior Luke Erb, a very competent shooter who was standing wide open in the left corner. As the pass was in the air, Triway's 6'10" post player, Sebastian Weber, frantically closed out from the paint to contest Luke's potential game-winning three-pointer.

From where I stood I couldn't tell for sure, but I believe Weber got a fingertip on the ball, because I could tell that it was right on line, but woefully short…

It's amazing the things a coach is capable of remembering in a very short period of time. I say this because as that ball was in the air, I had a second to think how rotten it was going to be when that ball ticked the front of the rim and fell off as the buzzer sounded. We had come so far from being a group of undersized, over-matched, ninth and tenth graders to the formidable opponent we were that night in challenging the two-time, defending state *Division-II Runners-up* in the *District*

Championship Game. I remember having time to think it was going to be tough to come so close and fall short, then have to say goodbye to the three seniors who had stuck with me *through thick and thin,* and a 3-31 start to their careers, without accomplishing our goal of winning a district.

...Just as I feared, Luke Erb's shot did fall short, scraping the front of the rim; however, what I hadn't realized is that we had advanced the ball so efficiently that the buzzer had not sounded as the ball was falling off the rim. With Weber standing in the corner after contesting Erb's shot, Brian Cross, who had been running down the center of the floor while the ball was being advanced, was left to go to the backboard unimpeded. As the crowd created a din that would drown out the sound of the buzzer, the ball fell straight into the hands of Cross—who was standing directly under the hoop—and he scooped it into the basket while being knocked out of bounds by Triway's fantastic forward, Jock Rottman. Then it got interesting.

When the ball went through the net, the Triway and Fairless crowds *both* broke into frenzied celebration—because each side thought it had won a district title: Triway, because the Titan fans thought the buzzer had sounded before Cross took the shot; Fairless, because our fans thought the shot by Cross beat the buzzer. And there was no immediate signal by any of the three officials, so nobody knew for sure.

In an ending that *Disney* might refuse on the principle that it seemed too contrived to make believable, there we were standing in the *Canton Memorial Field House* having scored what we thought *might have been* the basket that would send us to the *Division-II "Sweet-16"* just twenty-six months after the very same core of kids had been 0-12. But thirty-two minutes of regulation, plus four minutes of overtime, hadn't been enough to settle the issue.

The decision had gone to the jury—the three officials, who had done a tremendous job of keeping order in a very hotly-contested game, now huddled to decide whether the basket would count or not. After about fifteen seconds—which seemed like fifteen minutes—the lead official trotted over to the scorer's table, raised his hand and, as the crowd held its collective breath for a split second, emphatically waived it toward the floor signaling that the basket was *good. District Champs!* *"Sweet-16"! Rebuilding completed!*

Of course the official's signal set off a wild celebration that sent our student section onto the floor to mob our players and—because I was in complete awe of the scene—I really don't know what I did at first. I remember kind of raising my arms in the air and just watching the scene for a few seconds while a few people jumped on me on the way by. Then—like Jim Valvano *circa* 1983—I started looking for someone to hug. In my search, I made my way down toward the baseline where my wife, Chris, and family were sitting, and I was mobbed by my wife, my mom, my dad, and my uncle, Charlie Izzo. In this profession, a coach never knows when his finest moment or fondest memory is going to come. No matter how long I coach, that might very well have been mine.

Like I said, I couldn't resist going into the details of that game. I said early on in my introduction that sharing experiences and stories that may be of interest and of help to other coaches would be at the heart of this book. I think just about any coach who has ever had to take on a rebuilding project would find the ending of this story inspiring. Here were five kids—Brian Cross, Jonah Manack, Luke Erb, Jordan Jennings, and Josh Penland—all of whom started their varsity basketball careers losing in a big way, and all of them had a hand in the last possession that led to Brian Cross' shot that will be remembered forever in the lore of Fairless basketball. Beyond all the good work a coach does to help his players become solid people, isn't that a moment we all coach to experience?

The other reason I shared this story in so much depth is because it goes to the heart of my point in this section: My system of play evolved over a period of time to fit the needs of my program. We were not having success beating the better programs at *their* game, so we decided to create *our own game*, and the game became known as *Run & Stun*.

The system started by spreading the floor in the half court and aligning in a two-guard front with many of the concepts we run; the next step was the commitment to attacking offensively immediately upon gaining possession. The final piece was getting the players to work toward mastering the skills that went with those concepts so that we were performing together at a high level. *My best-laid plans—Run & Stun*—evolved out of the necessity for me to put my players in the best position I could to help them succeed. I sold it and taught it; they bought it and won. That's what *X's & O's* are all about, whether it's with a *Run & Stun* approach, a half-court approach, or somewhere in between—finding a system which fits personnel that a coach is capable of teaching at a high level so that the players can master its concepts and fundamental skills well enough to perform with high aptitude.

12
Parting Shots:
The power of coaching

500 (Montgomery)

FAMILY IS SO important in every life, but especially in a coaching family. My mother Helen and father Charles provided me with love, albeit tough love at times, and encouraged me *to chase my love—coaching*. Money was *always* an issue growing up, but somehow my parents found a way to get my brother and me through college. One of my favorite words is perseverance, and my mom and dad were certainly the driving force behind *my* perseverance as I earned my college education, started my career, and began the most important thing in my life—my family.

I mention my wife, Becky, many times in the book, and I mentioned the pride I have in my oldest daughter, Annie, as she has begun her coaching career. But I am equally proud of my other two daughters: Erin, a communications major at Malone University; and Leigh, our 18-year-old, severely-handicapped angel.

On top of all the hourly commitment that was at stake in my career, my wife had the added responsibility of raising a special needs child. Leigh has had eighteen brain surgeries—but she also has been to over 500 basketball games in her lifetime. That alone indicates how strong a family we have and the support I have enjoyed. As I have continuously mentioned throughout the book, I have been very fortunate.

100 (Kramer)

Hey, I don't even try to hide it—winning the *Canton Division-II District Championship* was an extremely special moment in my life because of everything it represented to me. First off, it was the triumphant culmination of a complete rebuilding project at Fairless that began in the summer of 2003—a job I undertook with a group of young men whom I truly grew to love through our struggles together. Anyone who watched those four years unfold understands why I had *"Sweet-16"* embroidered on everything I owned except my boxer shorts. (I couldn't find anyone to do it on my boxers.) As I said, the renaissance of my program was a real-life rags-to-riches story—complete with the *Disney* ending.

But winning the Canton District has also been kind of a life quest for my family. As an assistant, my father, Dan Kramer, was on a Hoban staff that beat Orrville in the 1978 *Canton AA District Championship Game* to make Hoban's first *"Sweet-16"* in school history. When that happened, I was eight years old—just old enough to really understand the excitement that was being generated by the tournament run. The night Hoban won that championship in 1978, I watched the celebration, and like many other kids who play basketball in Northeast Ohio, I vowed that someday I would climb the ladder and cut down the nets in the *Canton Memorial Field House.*

I also remember going to the regional game in 1978 at the *Canton Civic Center* and seeing the bright lights of the city and the arena atmosphere that was the venue. I remember asking my grandfather that night if he thought I'd ever get to be in a game in that arena. I don't remember his exact words, because it was a long time ago, but I remember his message to me was that he suspected I would. I honestly think he told me that because it was obvious to him that I was singularly focused on basketball, even at that very young age. Remembering that conversation with my grandfather in 1978 made making it to a regional in the Civic Center in 2007 a little bit more special.

About eighteen months after Hoban lost that regional game in 1978—in the spring of 1979—my dad became the head coach at Akron Hoban, and his goal was to win the Canton District again. Dan Kramer coached some very good teams in his four years as the head coach at our alma mater, most notably his 1982 team that fell just short of the district championship game—a team led by future 400-meter, world record holder and Olympic gold medalist, Butch Reynolds. In my dad's four years at Hoban his path to a *"Sweet-16"* was blocked by a couple great Orrville teams coached by the late legendary Steve Smith, and by the St. Vincent-St. Mary teams of Curtis Wilson and Jerome Lane, two players who would go on to play basketball at Ohio State and Pitt respectively. (Lane also actually went on to play a number of years in the NBA, most notably with the Denver Nuggets.)

After the 1982-83 season, my dad stepped down as the head coach when I entered Hoban High School as a freshman, and I picked up the quest from there—as a player. In 1986, as a junior, I was part of a

Hoban team that made it to the *Canton AA District Championship Game* by beating Coach Montgomery's first great Triway team in the District semi-finals. In the championship game, we fell short against another of Steve Smith's terrific Orrville teams in a very close game.

My senior season at Hoban we were knocked out of the tournament by a St. Vincent-St. Mary team that eventually went to the *Final Four*, so my playing days ended short of the goal. At that point, I thought winning the district was going to have to be chalked up as a goal left unattained, because I obviously had no idea the way my career path would wind at the time. As it turned out, the quest was far from over.

Ten years later, I actually had my first chance to climb those *Field House* ladders in the late 1990's as an assistant on Henry Cobb's staff at Canton South when we won the 1997 *Canton Division-II District Championship*—Ohio went from a three-class system to a four-division system in 1988. That was a great moment, certainly, and I loved it. But it was nothing compared to putting *my* stamp on *my own program* and winning my first *Canton Division-II District Championship* as a head coach in 2007 with those terrific kids from Fairless. Like I said, it was a great night to be able to share with Jonah Manack, Brian Cross, Luke Erb, Jordan Jennings, Josh Penland, Garret Manack, Josh Brinley, and their teammates that joined them over the years. But it was even more special to be able to share it with my dad.

I have spent a book in these pages giving credit to Henry Cobb, Randy Montgomery and many of the other excellent coaches who influenced my career. However, nobody was a bigger influence on me than my father, Dan Kramer. He was my idol when I was growing up, simple as that. He was always busy with work as a private contractor—my dad was not a teacher—but he was never too busy to swing by our house, pick me up, and take me to his practices. My brother Steve and I were always in that gym with our dad and his teams; we lived in that gym at Hoban—just as my oldest son, Luke, and daughter, Olivia, have lived in the gyms at Canton South and Fairless with me. Without a doubt, those early days made me the father and coach I am today.

When my 2007 team won the Canton Division-II District, it was for my dad as much as it was for me. Try as I might have, until now, I'm not sure I have ever been able to effectively make him understand that. I climbed the ladder that night because of the will he instilled in me to push my team to get there, and at our banquet at the end of the 2007 season, I presented him with a "Sweet-16" plaque that read, *"We did it"*, at the bottom. The fact of the matter is, without my dad I never would have pushed through the tough times to get it done.

Beyond my will to win championships, my dad also instilled in me the type of coach I am today—a coach who cherishes the relationships he creates with his players. When I was growing up, I remember my dad's players would always stay in contact with him, swing by the house at gatherings, and basically become a part of our extended family. In fact, when Butch Reynolds got off the plane after returning home from winning his gold medal at the 1992 Olympics in Seoul, Korea, my dad—his high school basketball coach—was the first person Butch hugged after he had hugged his own father. That always struck me as a really special aspect of my dad's job, and I always thought I would want it to be that way if I were ever a head coach.

Here's where I want to try and stress the weight of influence we carry as head coaches with one final story:

In early summer of 2009, I received a very random text message on the morning of June 7; it read: *Love you, man! You helped me get this far. You and the letter of recommendation you wrote for me that got me my scholarship. You helped me be who I am today.*

The text was from my former player, Elijah Desmond, the lone senior on my 2005 Fairless High School basketball team that won only four games. The message had actually been sent the night before, but I had fallen asleep in my recliner with my four-year-old son Luke on my chest watching *Titanic* on a cable station, and I didn't get it until I woke up the next morning. Of course the message made me feel good, so I shot a thank you back to Elijah right away and asked him if he would be in town for a few days so we could get out and have some wings and catch up a little bit.

Elijah responded back to me in a text: *"I'd like to do that before I leave for Hawaii on the eighth."*

I assumed Elijah meant June eighth, which would have been the next day, so I responded by asking him how long he would be in Hawaii. I wanted to know when he would return from his trip so I could get together with him when he came back into town. He quickly shot a text back in response that said: *"July 8th. And, oh, I'll be gone for a long time. I got a full-time job in Honolulu on Waikiki Beach!"*

Needless to say, Elijah is a kid that used his basketball experience to supplement his academic experience, and I really believe that he may be the best example I have of a former player that really understood what sports is supposed to teach kids.

This was not a player who played for a championship team. Elijah is the young man who came to my basketball program because he had to give up a wrestling career—one that was destined to land him a college scholarship—because of a rare spinal condition. Elijah's is a story of overcoming disappointment, staying humble, working hard, persevering, and driving to accomplish goals. Every coach would like to create a winning basketball factory—I'm no different. But whether we accomplish that goal or not, the life victories of a kid like Elijah, although they will never draw 5,000 people into a gymnasium and create a media frenzy, are more important in the greater scheme of things.

Elijah's success story has allowed him to stop and cut down the nets of life before he attacks the next opportunity that his journey presents him. The fact that he stopped to thank me—his former basketball coach—for any influence I may have had on him along the way was a very powerful reminder to me how important my job is.

The best-laid plans of any coach should be geared toward winning basketball games—no doubt about it. But on a grander scale those plans should also be geared toward leading young people. I think that is a responsibility coaches should take pretty seriously—a fact I am always reminded of when I receive a text or phone call from a former player.

With that, Randy Montgomery and I would both like to wish all of our readers luck in their coaching and leadership endeavors—we hope many of the ideas and stories presented in *The Best-Laid Plans of a High School Basketball CEO* provide support in every leader's pursuit of excellence.

CPSIA information can be obtained
at www.ICGtesting.com
Printed in the USA
BVHW092306270219
541404BV00001B/184/P

9 781457 508080